ENJOYING THE JOURNEY OF LIFE

BY MELANIE ROACH
U.S. OLYMPIAN

Advanced Praise for Enjoying the Journey

Endorsements

"As a teammate, competitor, and friend of Melanie from 1997-2000 I saw firsthand some of the ups and downs of her weightlifting career. I watched as she became the first US woman to clean and jerk double body weight, and also saw the tears and heartbreak after she didn't make the 2000 Olympic team. Melanie is such a talented lifter so I was extremely happy to see her dream come true when she made the 2008 Olympic Team. I am amazed at how she was able to accomplish that while raising 3 young children, one with autism, and while running a business. Her performance at the 2008 Olympic Games is an example of her determination, work ethic, her never-give-up attitude and her ability to persevere in difficult situations."

Tara Nott Cunningham
2000 Olympic Gold Medalist
2 time Olympian

"I've worked with countless champion Olympians over the course of my career but Melanie stands out even among the best of the best. While her remarkable physical strength will capture your attention, it's her extraordinary strength of character that will capture your heart. Her path to the Olympic Games was wrought with challenges, but she overcame them all with her eternally positive attitude, through her faith and family, and always with a beaming smile. Melanie is a woman from whom we can all draw strength."

Patrick Quinn
Partner, Chicago Sports & Entertainment Partners

"Melanie's story of passion and hard work, and her commitment to push herself farther every day to become among the best in the world is truly inspiring. Her drive and persistence serve as a shining example to all of us that if we work hard, we can all fulfill our dreams."

U.S. Representative, Dave Reichert
(Washington State, 8th Congressional District)

"Of all of the many attributes an athlete may possess, indeed that any of us may possess, integrity is the most important. Melanie Roach is the whole package. She has that highest goal. She has integrity."

State Senator, Pam Roach
(Washington State, 31st District)

"When I first met Melanie as part of our series of Olympic profiles on NBC News' "Today Show" in 2008, her inspiring tale of triumph immediately separated itself from the field. Her perseverance is proof for all of us that success is possible when you stay focused and true to yourself."

Peter Alexander
NBC News Correspondent

"I had a front row seat to Melanie's entire journey to reach the Olympics and her potential. Possessed of unique talent, she added in great drive and determination to become one of the best in the world. Though she faced many "road blocks", she perservered as few others are capable of doing, and she reached an amazing culmination of desire and work ethic to compete in Beijing 2008. It was a pleasure for me to share her journey."

John Thrush
Coach to Melanie Roach
Owner, Thrush Sports Performance

Lift: Enjoying The Journey of Life
ISBN: 978-0615692869

RGI Publising
1627 45th St E #D-103
Sumner, WA 98390

www.melanieroach.com

Cover and Interior Design: Lisa Garrison
Cover, Chapter 10, and Epilogue Photos: Erin Perkins Photography
All other photos: Roach family and friends

To my husband, Daniel,
And my three eldest children, Ethan, Drew and Camille.
You sacrificed the most to make my
Olympic dream a reality.

To my Autistic son, Drew.
Every challenge I face pales in comparison to what you
face each day. You teach me patience and perspective.

To all of my children, including my
post-Olympic additions, Charlie and Lily.
I hope you will be inspired from the experience as well!

Acknowledgments

To my Heavenly Father – for the power of faith, prayer, and for blessing me both physically and mentally to successfully meet this challenge. May I use all that I learned to benefit the lives of others, including my own children.

To my husband and best friend, Daniel – for your support, unselfishness, sacrifice, and unconditional love. For taking such great care of our children, for never letting me give up, and especially for pushing me out of the bed to finish my core exercises when I was too tired to do it on my own. I couldn't have done it without you!

To my children Ethan, Drew, and Camille – for allowing Mommy to pursue her dream of becoming an Olympian. I look forward to watching you follow your own dreams.

To my mother, Bonnie – for the incredible sacrifices you made, for the vital role you played in keeping our house running in the months and years prior to Beijing. Thank you for sacrificing both time and money to help me pursue my athletic dream of being a gymnast. The hours you spent sitting on a hard bench watching me train will never go unnoticed. Had you not made that sacrifice I would NOT be an Olympian or own a gymnastics gym.

To my father, Marshall and stepmother, Susan – thank you for teaching me a strong work ethic and for supporting me in all of my athletic endeavors.

To my in-laws, Jim and Senator Pam Roach – for raising such an incredible man whom I am lucky enough to call my husband. And yes, Pam, he is STILL PERFECT!

To my coach, John Thrush – for believing in me, for helping me believe in myself, and for teaching me to savor every minute and enjoy the process. Thank you for pushing me when I needed to be pushed and for holding me back when I needed to be held back. Thank you for sending me to Beijing prepared and for peaking me perfectly! Still hard to believe… 6 for 6 and a new American Record at 33 years of age! You are the master of preparation!

To my chiropractor, Dr. Greg Summers of Summers Chiropractic and Massage – for keeping these old bones young, for staying positive through the uncertainty of my back injury, and for sacrificing both time and money to make sure I was in tip-top shape at every competition no matter how far we had to travel. A special thank you to his wife, Leanne, for allowing her hubby to make his athletes a priority in the early years of establishing their business. I'll never forget the twice-baked lasagna!

To my back surgeon, Dr. Robert Bray of the D.I.S.C Center – for providing a way when it seemed all doors had closed on my dream. Because of your incredible care and precision, we were back in action in record time. Thank you for saving the dream!

To my nutritionist, Eleanor Barrager – for keeping my body fine tuned and firing on all cylinders. I learned so much from you. Thank you for sharing your brilliance!

To my agent, Patrick Quinn – who is an endless supporter, promoter and the reason we were able to hurdle the financial burden of going to the Olympics in an obscure sport.

To my friend and hair stylist, Marv Smith – for your support and friendship and for keeping me looking "cutting edge."

To my training partners, Lea Rentmeister, Rachel Churchward, Katie Thrush and Alexis Reed. I could always count on your support. You kept me motivated through thick and thin. Thank you for keeping me motivated to the end!

To Tracy Fober of Iron Maven – your state of the art technology put things into perspective and helped me tweak the lifts to gain every kilo possible right up to the finish in Beijing. Thank you for coming out to Seattle.

To my manager, Melanie Johndrow, and the rest of my staff at Roach Gymnastics – thank you for taking the reins at a critical point in my preparation.

To Dr. Bruce and Julie Molen – for ongoing support beginning in the early years of my career. A special thank you for introducing me to my sweet husband.

To my siblings. My sister Vicky for being such a great example of hard work. My brother Kordell – for turning me into a tough girl who was never afraid of a little pain and a HUGE thank you for your generosity in making sure Coach Thrush made it to China! And to my brother Christopher for helping me strengthen my perspective on perseverance.

To Bishop David Wagner – for his inspired council that helped me apply the power of perspective!

To former WA Secretary of State, Ralph Munro – thank you for your genuine and heartfelt support towards me and my family.

To Dr. David Molen- for your generous support during the final stretch leading up to the Olympics.

To my friends in the community – for the incredible community support from both the cities of Bonney Lake and Sumner. The rally at Allan York Park will go down as one of my fondest memories. Thank you for the heartfelt support!

To my sponsors – McDonalds, Summer's Chiropractic and Massage, D.I.S.C. Center, BioEnergy Ribose, Hat Trick Beverages, Iron Maven, QSports, Molen Oral Surgery, Lara Bar and Solstix Jerky.

And finally, I wish to convey my great appreciation to Molly Venzke, a professional writer, who organized my thoughts and helped convert them to the written word.

Table of Contents

Forward

"Allen, you have to come see these children."

That was one of the first things Melanie Roach told me when we made contact in Beijing. I was there to cover the 2008 Olympics, she was there to compete. Neither one of us had much time for anything other than the job at hand. Or so I thought.

I knew immediately she was serious and I knew immediately it meant I was going to see "these children", whoever and wherever they were, at some point very soon. Whether it was advisable as a visiting reporter in China or not... You CAN say "no" to Melanie Roach, but it really won't do you much good.

So a few days after she proved herself the fifth-best woman on the planet in her sport, she led photographer Ken Jones and me out of the city and into semi-rural suburbs to a small home inside a walled courtyard. And we met "these children".

It was an orphanage of sorts, a half-way house for desperately sick children. They were waiting for help, for medical treatment their parents hadn't been able to afford or that simply wasn't available in their smaller cities and villages. And they were waiting and hoping for a new life, for new parents, for love.

Melanie was right; I had to come see these children. They are faces, eyes, tiny hopeful souls I will never forget. They are reminders of the world beyond deadlines and political campaigns and gang-shootings; beyond the flags and trumpets and gold and glory of the Olympic games.

I don't remember how she heard about the place. But here's the point: with all that was going on in her life, with the achievement of a lifelong dream at hand, with the demands of her sport and her team and her family and an autistic son... while all the million moving parts that comprise an Olympic games spinning around her, Melanie was thinking instead about these children. And she made us come visit with our equipment and tell their story to the world. And for that I will always be thankful.

That's Melanie Roach. An athlete devoted to her sport but far more devoted to her faith and her husband and her children. And those other children. Any other children.

Enjoy the book. It was written by a tough, tiny woman who can lift twice her body-weight, and who has a heart big enough for all the children of the world.

Allen Schauffler
NBC News Anchor
KING 5 Evening News, Seattle

One:
The Olympic Dream

*Melanie, with her signature smile, after a successful 242 lbs
"clean and jerk" at the 2008 Olympics.*

Chapter One:

THE OLYMPIC DREAM

IT WAS A BIG RISK. But it was a chance of a lifetime, so it was a risk I was willing to take. Here I was representing my country in the Beijing 2008 Summer Olympics, an experience that only a tiny percentage of Americans would ever have; how could I not walk in the opening ceremonies? The only problem was, in less than 36 hours, I would be in the thick of competing, and in order to do my very best, I needed to stay off my legs as much as possible. But by the same token, I felt that walking in the opening ceremonies with Team USA was almost as much a part of participating in the Olympics as actually competing. Ever since I could remember, I'd watch these opening ceremonies on the television and feel my heart yearning for the day that I, too, might be walking proud in my red, white and blue.

And so, at the very last second, I outfitted myself in my official United States of America 2008 Olympic uniform, jumped on a bus that was filled with other Team USA athletes, and rode out towards the opening ceremony's venue. The bus took us straight to the Gymnastics Stadium, which served as a holding tank for us, as well as the thousands of other world athletes. They lined us up country by country, in alphabetical order, and there we all waited for our country's turn to be led to Beijing's National Stadium, colloquially known as "the Bird's Nest," and walk in the opening parade.

By now, it was evening and the sky was mostly dark, but make no mistake: nighttime in Beijing during the summer can still be incredibly hot! The temperature was a whopping 95 degrees with high humidity, and the smog was thick enough to slice. There were 596 athletes in the US delegation, and we were all in our identical Ralph Lauren designed outfits of long, cream-colored pants, a navy blazer over a long-sleeved white shirt, a red, white and navy striped scarf, and a white pageboy cap. We certainly looked sharp and classically American, but we also were very, very hot. I laugh now when I think about

Team USA, standing there waiting for nearly five hours, totally overdressed, and sweating like crazy. I decided that, rather than allowing doubts to enter my mind that maybe I'd have been better off resting back at the Olympic Village, I should try and pass the time by walking around and meeting other US athletes.

Finally, it was the United States' turn to enter the stadium. The entirety of Team USA zigzagged from the Gymnastics Stadium towards the National Stadium, and was led to a tunnel, very similar to the inclined tunnel of a football stadium. It was from here that we'd enter the arena. The atmosphere was electric, and by now I was so filled with anticipation, I'd forgotten how hot it was. Because of the upward slope, I could see an enormous American flag waving at the entry point, and just before Team USA was to begin spilling out into the stadium, all 596 of us began chanting, "USA! USA! USA!" The sound of our unison voices made my body tingle with emotion, and all I could think about was how incredibly proud I was to be an American.

I was walking near the back of the team, and not being one of our taller athletes, I couldn't see over the hundreds of team members in front of me. But the closer I came to the mouth of the tunnel, the louder the chanting became, until I emerged into the vast open stadium. It took my breath away to hear the thunderous chants from the 91,000 spectators as they, too, were shouting in unison: "USA! USA! USA! USA!"

There are no words to fully describe how it felt to walk around that stadium, waving to people from all over the world, as I represented my nation at the 2008 Summer Olympics. I breathed in the moment, looked into the stands, and smiled at as many people as I could make eye contact with. This was, without a doubt, the most patriotic experience of my life...and well worth any risk of being on my legs so much before a competition. However, because of the closeness of my event, I knew I couldn't be careless, and I took what was called the "opt out" route. This meant one lap around the stadium, and then immediately exiting and taking the bus back to the Olympic village. That night I fell asleep to the background noise of fireworks coming from the evening's 4-hour long Opening Ceremonies, so happy I'd made the choice to be a participant.

The next morning, I woke up fully focused for my competition the following day. My body felt great, although I have to admit, my eyes were so swollen from being out in the smog the night before, I looked like I'd been punched in the face! But other than this, I was well rested, and in my mind, completely at peace.

Because I had packed ample amounts of food, I didn't have to walk the long (and sweltering hot) distance to the cafeteria. I was able to relax in my dorm room the entire day as I watched Season 3 of the television series, 24, for 8 consecutive hours. This was a strategy I'd concocted the previous year at the 2007 World Championships. Those episodes of Jack Bauer, hour by hour saving the country, are so intense my mind doesn't have the space to think, or more accurately, to over-think the lifting I needed to do for the competition. Since this tactic had worked well for me at the World Championships, I stuck with it for the Olympics. So the day flew by, and thanks to Jack, I felt no nerves, and that night I slept like a baby.

My first impression when I opened my eyes the next morning was how void I was of the usual pre-competition jitters. I felt entirely clothed in peace with the confidence that I had done absolutely everything in my power to prepare for this day. I had no regrets, and I couldn't wait to experience this pinnacle in my weightlifting career. Before eating, I went to check my weight, which was right where it needed to be at 53kgs (117lbs). I returned to my room to shower, style my hair, apply my make-up, and put on my USA uniform and my earrings. I said a prayer of thanks to God, and placed the day's events into His hands. Only then did I leave my room to board the shuttle that took me to the Beihang University Gymnasium, the 5,400 seat indoor arena where the weightlifting competitions were being held.

After my official weigh in, I ate a breakfast of oatmeal, drank a Gatorade, and waited for the competition to begin. Still, I felt no jitters, just a bit of giddy disbelief that I was actually at the Olympic Games. My assigned Olympic coach, however, was showing his nervousness as he was attaching my number on my uniform with his shaky, fumbling hands; I thought for sure he was going to poke me with one of the pins. I don't think the reality of my situation completely hit me until they called all the athletes out for a "walk in," and we all lined up to parade out onto the platform. There was a huge Olympic banner, the packed arena was cheering wildly, and when the announcer called my name and country, I saluted with pride. In addition, I was blessed to be able to decipher the shouts from my family and key members of Team Roach in the stands. That was a tremendous feeling to hear their support and to know I was sharing this moment, not only with my entire country, but also with the people whom I hold dearest to my heart.

Now it was game time. I put on my iPod, focused my mind, and got into 'the zone.' All I had to do was walk out there and repeat a process that I'd done thousands of times. I played it over and over in my mind, perfect lift after perfect lift. I could hear the voice of my personal coach, John Thrush, echoing through my head, 'Stay over the bar, keep your back tight, and your elbows out.' After several minutes, I felt my Olympic coach tap my shoulder to let me know my turn was up to perform the first portion of the competition, the "snatch" lift. This was my moment of a lifetime.

For those of you who are unfamiliar to weightlifting, the snatch lift is one coordinated, continuous movement that is executed with speed. Without going into the extreme complexities of this technique, in the snatch, the lifter approaches the barbell by squatting down and gripping the bar with a very wide overhand grip. In an aggressive pull up, the lifter brings the weight above her head with locked out arms while positioning her body in a low squat. Once the weight is secure overhead, the lifter squats up into a standing position. Obviously, I had performed this lift more times than I could count, and my body felt ready to perform at its peak.

I took off my iPod, strode to the edge of the platform and chalked up my hands at the chalk dish. As I heard Team Roach yelling for me, I took a mental snapshot. This was not just ordinary chalk clouding upwards as I covered my hands; this was Olympic chalk! I approached the weight, squared my feet, and tightened my lifting belt. Stay over the bar, keep your back tight, and your elbows out, I rehearsed in my mind. Reaching down to the bar, I settled my grip and then pulled it off the ground straight over my head. I stood up and held it steady until the judges gave me the signal of a good lift by illuminating their three white lights. I smiled broadly, dropped the weight, and acknowledged the cheers before returning to the warm-up area.

In competition, making your first lift is a huge mental hurdle. Not only does it fill you with confidence, but also, if that first lift is successful, then you are allowed to move up in weight and go for the "big lifts." On the other hand, if you miss that crucial lift, your entire strategy is blown, and in many cases, so is your confidence. In this debut lift at the 2008 Olympics, I'd made my first lift with such ease that my confidence soared and I knew I was capable of bigger weights with my next attempts.

In the end, I was successful in all three "snatch" lifts! 79kgs (173.8lbs), 81kgs (178.2lbs), and 83kgs (182.6lbs), with 83kgs being my all-time personal best! I was exhilarated, to say the least, and I smiled ear-to-ear in the direction of Team Roach's exuberant cheers. But then, I had to quickly squelch my excitement for the time being because in only 15 minutes, the second portion of the competition, the "clean and jerk" lifts, would begin.

Again, to explain in laymen's terms, the clean and jerk lift is different from the snatch. This is a lift where the barbell is picked up from the floor and placed on the shoulders in one, "clean" motion. After a pause, the athlete moves to the second stage of the motion, the "jerk." Here, the athlete lifts the barbell into an overhead position while placing the legs in a lunge. Once secure, she lunges up to a full standing position.

During the break, I knew I needed to get back into my zone and reenergize myself for the next set of lifts. I ate a bit more and listened to my iPod. I began to visualize perfect lift after perfect lift. Once again, I felt my coach's tap on my shoulder to signify my turn in the competition. I steadily walked out onto the platform feeling even more razor-sharp-focused than before. I chalked up, and took my stance over the bar.

All three of my clean and jerk attempts were successful! 105kgs (231lbs), 107kgs (235.4lbs), and 110kgs (242lbs). At the 2008 Beijing Olympics, I had just gone 6 for 6, which is very rare in weightlifting competitions, especially at this level. It was an American Olympic record! And on top of that, once the total weight from my two best lifts were calculated, I had earned not only a new personal all-time best score, but also, I had set a new American record for my weight class! I felt ecstatic, and I couldn't wipe the smile off my face. One would've thought I'd just won the gold medal, rather than a very respectable 5th place.

Obviously, every Olympic athlete would love to win a gold, silver or bronze; but honestly, even if I had won a medal, I'm not sure my level of fulfillment or happiness could've been any higher. Because *personally*, at these 2008 Olympic Games, not only had I performed at 100% of my ability as I achieved successful scores at the biggest meet of my life, but I had also had the opportunity to finish something that had actually started 11 years ago. I was able to right some wrongs, to write a new ending to my career, and clean out some of the old skeletons that had been lurking around in my closet from earlier in my career.

You see, back in 1997, when they announced that women's weightlifting was going to premiere at the 2000 Olympics, I was supposed to be on that team. I was even projected to go for the gold. And while my talent and my physical body might have been up for that task, my mental and emotional stamina had not quite reached the maturity required to compete at such a level. Leading up to the 2000 Olympics, I ended up bombing out at crucial meets, almost eliminating all chances at securing a spot on the team. As a result, I had to claw my way back from these defeats by competing in other meets to put myself back in the position to qualify. And then, just weeks before the Olympic trials, my back was crippled with a herniated disc, subsequently causing me to lose any chance to be on the 2000 Olympic team. Then in 2003, I tried to make a comeback for the 2004 games only to have the same terrible back injury flare up and take me out of the running. In all respects, it seemed as though my dream to compete in the Olympics was totally out of my reach.

That 11-year span from 1997-2008 had been a cycle of extreme highs, and extreme lows. I had walked through a series of failures, some personal ones and some major public ones. In addition, I'd faced several very painful injuries and setbacks in my physical body, and even more overwhelmingly, the emotional setback of discovering my second son was suffering from autism. But before you go grab a tissue, I also want to stress that these years weren't only sad. I had also enjoyed some of my life's greatest highlights, like: meeting my husband, Dan, building a strong marriage followed by the births of our three children, successfully founding a thriving gymnastics school, and working to see Dan win a seat in our state's legislature. And perhaps most importantly, those years taught me invaluable lessons and shaped me into the woman I am today.

So in 2008, as I stood in the Beihang University Gymnasium, having just successfully completed 6 for 6, as well as setting American and personal records, the taste of victory was indescribably sweet. This experience was a culmination of those 11 years, a climax of achievement for me personally, emotionally, mentally, physically, and publicly. It was a pinnacle stop in my journey of life; obviously, not an end, but a very profound moment in time that represented me making it to the summit of a long, uphill battle.

And this is why I write this book. Not because I made a surprise comeback to go to the Olympics, or that I hit 6 for 6, or even that I set new American records. While those facts are a part of my story, in reality, they're only a very small part. No, I write because, just like you, I know what it's like to face extreme adversity. I understand how it feels to have every fiber of my being crying out to throw in the towel and give up. And I realize how difficult it is to keep on keeping on when life throws its curve balls. Trust me, I'm no different from you. I have the same hang-ups, and the same insecurities.

But I also have found several strategies to lift myself up out of the pit and win anyway. I've discovered a recipe for life that has helped me move from depressed to joyful, from exhausted to energized, from being defeated to being a champion. *Lift: Enjoying the Journey of Life* is the recipe, and with each chapter, I'll give you a new "ingredient" that will build on the one before. Let me assure you, it is only because of the principles I'm about to share with you in these subsequent chapters that I was able to come to a place of internal fortitude and stand on that Olympic platform. And I'm confident that if you allow the insights from this book to penetrate your life, there is no obstacle you cannot overcome.

Many times when a person sees another become very successful, I have heard them say, "Wow. That guy is so lucky to have been able to achieve so much. I wish I was that lucky." But the reality is, the reason most people become successful in a particular area has absolutely nothing to do with luck. Rather, their success is built slowly over a period of time by making a lot of small, good choices each and every day. Mine certainly wasn't overnight; my Olympic journey was more than a decade in the making! And moreover, that journey was anything but perfect. It was filled with many trials and heartbreaks along the way. But the keys in this book helped me to lift above those heartbreaks; to persevere, to work hard, to overcome any obstacles, and to keep my eyes focused on the prize.

In fact, even during the process of writing this book, I cannot express to you how much these principles helped me! Coinciding with the months of this book project, I happened to go through more than one challenging season as well as a few major transitions in life. Both Dan and I had to make some key business decisions, and I was so thankful that the truths that this book contains were fresh in my heart and mind. They helped me to stay strong on the inside and to keep my outlook positive about what was happening around us. Because I followed my own advice, I was able to enjoy the journey of each day...even the difficult ones.

As you work through these chapters, I'd recommend you underline parts that ring true to you and inspire you, so they'll be easy to find at a later date. Go ahead and make notes in the margins. Write your thoughts and any strategies that pop in your mind about how to apply these truths to your own life. I've even included extra blank pages specifically for you to journal or to jot down revelations you are having about yourself as well as ideas about how to grow and change.

No matter where you are in life, no matter how old or how young, there are new adventures and new challenges that await you. My desire is that this book will help you to engage more fully with life, to learn to see the positive in every situation, and to motivate you to go for every single dream inside your heart. In a time when hope seems to be a far-off reality, I want to encourage you that if you can envision it, you can achieve it! And these old-fashioned rules of thumb, repackaged for the 21st century person, can help you win in every area of life. You can lift your life to any realm of success. You can do anything you set your mind to...anything at all. I know this book will help get you there.

Just pick a dream, and go for it!

Two:
The Power of Choice

"I'm more balanced, having the challenges of raising a family and running a business, and having an autistic child. Weightlifting is the easiest part of my day"

Chapter Two:
THE POWER OF CHOICE

They were the hardest words I had ever heard. As I sat on my couch looking into my mother-in-law's teary eyes, I could hardly believe what she'd just said. And out of all the days of the year, did she have to pick Christmas morning to drop this bomb? But I also knew how much she loved me, that she had our family's best interest at heart, and more importantly, that she'd weighed her words very heavily.

My only comfort was that I was sure she was mistaken. Drew, my two-year-old, had autism? No way. Yeah, he was a difficult child who randomly threw monumental temper tantrums, who wouldn't make eye contact, and who no longer seemed to respond to his name. But autistic? Dan and I were certain she was quite wrong on this one. And let's not even mention that as we sat together on that Christmas morning in 2004 (four years prior to my experience at the Olympics), I was seven months pregnant with baby #3, soon to be a mother of 3 children under 3 years of age! The last thing I was prepared to handle at this point was a child with autism.

The only reason I considered taking Drew in to be evaluated is because of my respect for my mother-in-law and I'd given her my promise that I would. When I called the specialist, I found there was a huge waiting list, and it wouldn't be until May that we could schedule an appointment. In the meantime, however, I made an appointment with Drew's regular pediatrician and I began to do my own research about autism. As I read article after article about autism, while I was still in denial that Drew actually had it, I definitely could understand why my mother-in-law had concerns. The signs were there.

I began to notice how Drew would sit in a chair and simply "space out" for long periods of time. Also, he'd spend copious amounts of time in the windowsill lining his cars up over and over and over. And when he'd play with his trains, he wouldn't actually "play" with his train-cars like a typical child would, rather, he'd simply lay on the ground and watch the wheels going round and round. But with all this, I rationalized that my son was simply a quirky kid who loved his cars and trains.

In March of 2004, I took Drew to his pediatrician. She asked me a few questions and then told me she didn't think he was autistic; she didn't see the usual signs. At first, I felt an enormous weight lift from my heart, but as I was leaving her office, I couldn't let go of the words my mother-in-law had said. After expressing more of my concerns with her, she answered, "Melanie, if you have a gut instinct that something might be wrong with Drew, then you really should follow it." Reluctantly, I went back into her office so she could write a referral to a speech pathologist, and I promptly went home and made the appointment.

The day of our meeting with the speech pathologist finally came. My mother, (Nana) and I went together with Drew to the evaluation, and we were directed to wait in a seating area until our names were called. After about

15 minutes, the speech pathologist greeted us and asked if we would all move into her meeting room. The only problem was we couldn't get Drew to make the short walk from the seating area into her office. All he would do was thrash on the floor in a full-throttle tantrum. The nice woman simply sat down and observed him.

"Is this how he normally handles change or social situations like this?" she asked. I answered that it was normal, to which she began taking notes.

Once we were able to coerce Drew to settle down and come with us into her office, she opened up a large area filled with all sorts of children's toys. She asked Drew if he'd like to play. He didn't respond to her, but he did go right for the trains and began to line them up one after another. Then he lay there, and started watching the wheels as they spun around and around on the carpet. She tried to get him to sit up, but he wouldn't. She tried to play with him, but he didn't respond to her. Then she reached out to touch one of the trains, and Drew began throwing a fit, stopping only if she pulled her hand away. Again and again, the doctor made attempts to engage with Drew, but it was all to no avail.

She turned her attention to us and began to ask us a string of questions. "Is this fairly typical?" Yes. "Does he respond to his name?" No, not really. "Does he give eye contact?" No, hardly ever. "Here is a long list of words; can you mark all the ones Drew says?" We were stunned we could only circle a total of ten words.

These were very difficult questions to endure because I began to realize Drew was not always this removed or unable to communicate. In fact, at one point, he was developing typically, even above average. When he had just turned 2 years of age, we discovered he had learned his entire alphabet, just by observing us working with his older brother, Ethan. In addition, he knew all of his animal sounds, he'd point to airplanes in the sky, he'd make eye contact and smile, and he *definitely* could say more than ten words. And now, as we sat looking at the long list of words, we could only honestly circle ten. Ten words! At that moment, it was glaringly obvious how far backwards our little Drew had regressed. I could feel my heart breaking.

After 30 minutes with this speech pathologist, she informed us that while Drew displayed all the signs for autism, she was unable to offer an official diagnosis. We would need to see a child psychologist in order to receive a final prognosis. She gave us a referral, and as I walked out of her office, I thought the last thing in the world I wanted to hear was an official diagnosis telling me my rambunctious little boy had autism. Yet at the same time, I knew we needed finality.

Once again, when I called to make the appointment with the child psychologist, there was a long wait to get in. As the receptionist threw out possible dates that were months away, a lump began forming in my throat. I couldn't bear to wait that long! Then suddenly by an extreme stroke of luck, while I was right there on the phone with her, there was a cancellation. We were able to see this doctor the very next day. I hung up the phone, closed my eyes, and offered up a prayer of thanks to God for making a way for us to get in so quickly.

At 10:30 am, Dan, Drew and I went in for a final analysis. This child psychologist was a very dry and serious man. We walked into his office, he observed Drew for about two minutes, and then very matter-of-factly, stated, "Oh, yes, I see this all the time, and his signs are very clear. Your son has autism; I'm sure of it." And with that, he pulled off a yellow post-it note, scribbled down a number, and handed it to me. "This is the number for the state's Birth to Three program."

The end. Our meeting with him was over. No instructions, no information, no explanation about what it meant to have autism, or how it affects the family, or what to expect for the future. Nothing. Well, except that our son officially had autism. We had the yellow sticky note to prove it.

You might be able to imagine our shock as well as our frustration. Perhaps you've found yourself in a situation like this before. For me at that moment, it felt as if the air had just been sucked out of the room, and there wasn't going to be a yellow oxygen mask deploying from the ceiling any time soon. Yes, it was good to finally have a final diagnosis, but it was still a huge blow to hear that my 2-year-old son had a severe case of autism.

And the weight upon my heart only continued to grow heavier as I began to immerse myself in the information to learn more about autism and the stark realities it presented. Without a miracle, he'd never really be able to articulate his feelings to anyone, or engage in creative discussions. He'd probably never learn to read or even be able to live outside the care of Dan and me. He would never drive, never be able to date and fall in love and get married, never feel the satisfaction of a successful career or the joy of raising his own children. As far as I was concerned, my son was trapped inside his own body, and he was never going to have the opportunity, the one that most of us take for granted, to truly live his life freely. The grief I felt for him was enormous, comparative only to the loss of a loved one, and I was totally uncertain about how to proceed.

SOMETHING'S GOT TO GIVE

Dan and I processed the news very differently, and our outward responses showed the contrast. Dan tried to see the positive in the situation. He loved Drew deeply, and receiving a diagnosis of autism didn't change that one bit. In fact, knowing Drew actually was a special needs child helped Dan become more patient with him. He was able to lower his expectations for Drew's behavior, so that when he threw another tantrum, or broke another lamp, or shrieked all night long, Dan would understand the reason behind it. Of course, there were times when my husband would be frustrated, but overall, he tried to keep his outlook on everything, optimistic. Dan's perspective allowed him to take the news in stride, to cruise along in "business as usual" mode, and most importantly, to move our family forward.

I was the opposite. I saw nothing positive about Drew's diagnosis. In fact, it seemed I could only dwell on the negative. I'd think about how difficult each day would be from here on out, and how the problems would only grow proportionally as my son grew bigger. I'd imagine (and mourn over) all the things he would never be able to do. Each day, I'd imagine how much of a negative impact this would have on our entire family, and each night, I'd kneel at the foot of Drew's bed and emphatically pray that God would heal him.

Because I tend to internalize my feelings, outwardly I didn't show a great deal of emotion; inwardly however,

I was spiraling downward. My coping mechanism was to work as hard as I could to 'cure' my son. I immersed myself in research and tried to unearth any therapy that might improve his condition. I became utterly obsessed, as I felt it would be irresponsible to leave any stone unturned to help Drew. Special Note: While I feel it is important for parents of special needs children to do all they can to help their kids so that they will never have any regrets, it is even more important for us parents to stay balanced in it all (again, more on this later). At this juncture, I was definitely *not* the picture of balance as I drove all over, in and out of state, to find the right therapy. In addition, we dropped thousands of dollars out-of-pocket to provide almost daily one-on-one sessions for Drew, hoping to facilitate improvement. I had become single minded, and had started to neglect everything else in my marriage, my other children, my household, my business, and my weightlifting training.

I have to admit how grateful I am that before entering this extraordinarily intense season, Dan and I had been so diligent to build a solid marriage foundation (I'll be sharing more about how to do that in a later chapter). For married couples dealing with the stress of a child with autism, the divorce rate is upwards of 90%. I'm convinced, had we not gone into these next difficult months with such a strong bond, our marriage could've ended up on the wrong side of that statistic.

Months of this went by, and I'm sure what I was experiencing internally began to manifest itself in my outward appearance. People began to actually see the burden on me; it was so heavy. And even though I wasn't talking about it to many people, my sadness and depression were impossible to hide. Both Dan and I were existing in survival mode, trying to keep up with everything, and just hanging on to the hope that very soon things would begin to get better. I knew something had to change, but in the midst of dog paddling to keep my head above water, I didn't have the time or the energy to figure it out.

Thank Goodness, Dan and I were not walking alone. In December of 2005, almost one year to the date my mother-in-law first addressed the issue of autism with me, something happened that altered the course of my life forever. It was a Sunday morning, and as usual, our family was going to church. Right after the service was over, I felt a tap on my shoulder. When I turned around, I was surprised to see my bishop's secretary. He had a kind look on his face as he asked, "The Bishop asked if he could speak with you for a moment in his office?" This was very unusual, because he normally didn't conduct interviews with people at that time. So, of course, I agreed, knowing whatever it was he wanted to talk to me about must be important.

As we walked into his office and sat down, I felt immediately at ease. We had known each other for a long time, and he knew my personal history well. Plus, he had always been a cheerful friend to encourage both Dan and me whenever we needed it. After we settled in, he looked across his desk and kindly asked, "How are you doing?"

Perhaps it was because of my trust for this man, or maybe because he'd caught me off-guard and hadn't given me the advance warning to put on my everything-is-OK face. Maybe it was a little bit of both. Either way, his words were like an ice pick hitting a faulty slope of snow, and in an avalanche of emotion, I completely broke down and began to sob. I couldn't help myself, and I released the tears of several months of stress and grief. After a few moments, I looked at him and said despairingly, "Bishop, I didn't sign up for this." I could tell by his expression he understood I was referring to Drew, his autism, and all that had come with it.

In his wisdom, he took a few moments to think about what I'd just said. And then he spoke the words that completely changed my perspective forever. He simply smiled at me and said, "Melanie, this is *exactly* what you signed up for." And then he sat back in his chair to allow the weight of his words sink into my heart.

For the next few seconds, I let that sentence reverberate in my mind. Each time I replayed it, the truth of it resonated louder and deeper in my soul. While I couldn't yet articulate how just that one sentence was doing a profound work on the inside of me, I knew the bishop was right. I thanked him for his time, and in a bit of a daze, left his office to find where Dan and my family were.

The rest of that afternoon, I couldn't get away from what the bishop had said, and after a few hours of rumination, I "got it," and the reality of his words finally hit me. Even though I was by myself at this exact moment, my eyes lit up and I said out loud, "Oh my goodness, what the bishop said is absolutely right! This *is* what I signed up for...it's *exactly* what I signed up for." Right then and there, I felt like a hundred pound weight had just been lifted off my shoulders.

At first read, you might not understand the entirety of the subtext behind that powerful statement, or why it affected me so much; let me explain. What the bishop's advice meant was, when I signed up for Life, when I entered into the adventure of this earth walk, I had agreed to everything that went with it: the good, the bad, and the ugly. The triumphs *and* the failures. The joys *and* the sorrows. The ease and the struggles. The children who progressed normally *and* the children who had special needs. I couldn't complain that "I didn't sign up for this," because every aspect of my life was *exactly* what I'd signed up for.

In addition, I've always been taught that God knows the intimate details in his children's lives, and that He would never allow me to face a situation without also providing the courage and the strength to overcome it. So no matter how difficult this particular challenge seemed, I couldn't tell myself "I can't handle this," or "This is just too hard for me," or even, "If only Drew would be healed, *then* we can all be happy again," because none of these statements are true. The fact is, I *can* handle this, it *isn't* too hard for me, and even if Drew never gets healed, we can *still* choose to be happy.

Like a light switch clicking from 'off' to 'on', I was suddenly able to see things from a different vantage point, and I had this epiphany: all I needed to do was change my perspective! Ever since that morning my mother-in-law sat me down to talk about Drew, I had chosen to view everything about the situation with a negative slant. Unlike Dan, who'd found the ability to see the positive, I'd *only* focused on the negative. Consequently almost a year later, I found myself depressed, tired, and under an enormous burden of defeat.

No more, I vowed to myself that Sunday afternoon. *From this day forward, I'm going to change my perspective! Instead of seeing everything through a filter of negativity and discouragement, I'm going to shift my focus to see the positive in every situation...and not just with Drew, but also in my entire life.*

On that Sunday morning, there was no way I could've foreseen how that one meeting with my bishop, and that one decision to change my perspective, would dramatically alter the course of my life forever. But now, as I look back almost seven years later, I can clearly see how this incident was a catalyst for so many great experiences and accomplishments to come.

YOU HAVE A CHOICE

The number one ingredient in the recipe for enjoying the journey of your life is a positive perspective. I cannot stress to you how vital this particular discipline is to experiencing success in every realm of your life. As you can see, I've devoted an entire chapter to this even *before* I began writing to you about how to enjoy the journey (and that is the subtitle of this book!). The truth is, if *Enjoying the Journey of Life* is the picture you desire for your future, then having a positive perspective is the hook upon which that picture hangs. And that hook's name is Choice.

Every single day, every single person has the opportunity to choose how they are going to respond to their circumstances and their world. Many times we are not in charge of what situations we might face from day to day, but we do have the power of choice. We can choose to have a positive perspective by seeing ourselves as the winner, or to have a negative perspective by seeing ourselves as the defeated. We can choose to allow conflict to sharpen our senses as we look for success, or we can choose to lay down and give up the fight. We can choose to see beauty and inspiration, or we can choose to see darkness and depression. Choice is *everything*, and as the old saying goes, "What you see is what you get!"

Before I met with the bishop, I felt completely overwhelmed by the nature of our situation with autism, and unable to bear the weight of it. My mindset each morning was focused on how difficult that day would be, and furthermore, each negative situation I encountered with Drew only proved my viewpoint to be true. Every broken glass, every ripped piece of furniture, every screaming tantrum only served to reinforce how "right" I was to feel so awful about our situation. But once the light bulb went on inside my head and I realized that I didn't *have* to feel this way, that I simply needed to make the choice to change my perspective, it was like I'd been moved from the backseat of a bus speeding recklessly downhill, to being in full command of the driver's seat.

And let me tell you, taking a firm grip on that steering wheel was amazing! Suddenly, I was director of my emotions, and my life stopped feeling like it was careening out of control. Instead of allowing the state of my mind and emotions to be dependent upon whatever good or bad events came upon me, I resolved to keep my perspective positive regardless of the situations. The result: I was no longer a victim of circumstance, and I began my journey of enjoying every day of my life. All because of an on-purpose choice.

No matter what situation you might be facing while you hold this book in your hands, let me assure you, you *can* begin to enjoy even the toughest of problems if you will make a quality decision to see things in a positive light. I realize this might not be the easiest thing to do; indeed, some days it's a choice you will have to make over and over again. But let me assure you, if you will press forward to look for the cloud's silver lining, your efforts will be well rewarded.

Are you unemployed? Then, work hard each day to find a job while you learn to enjoy the gift of time you've been given. Meet up with your spouse or child for lunch. Take a walk and smell the roses. Rediscover a long-lost hobby. Fix those pesky household projects that have been hanging over your head. Soon enough, you'll be back in the 9-to-5 grind, and you won't have the time to enjoy many of these things.

Have you lost a loved one? Nothing can take away the inevitable grief you are experiencing, but perhaps you can lessen the weight by turning your focus away from that grief and onto remembering the wonderful times you shared with that person.

Are you struggling in your marriage? What if you began to see your spouse through the lens of when you were first falling in love? Every day try to see just one good quality in your spouse and focus on that. In many cases, marriages can be turned around simply by a shift in perspective.

You *can* begin to see every situation, both good and bad, in a positive light. You just need to lift your vision upward and choose to see the silver lining. And when you do so, you will begin the process of enjoying the journey of life...even during the challenging seasons. Remember, each chapter will build on the previous one, so keep reading! By the end of this book, you will have an entire arsenal to use to have victory in every day of your life.

Three:
Enjoying the Journey

Melanie and Drew

Chapter Three:
ENJOYING THE JOURNEY

I WILL FOREVER BE INDEBTED to my bishop, not only for taking the time to notice how much I was struggling, but also for caring enough to meet with me on that Sunday morning. His words empowered me to rise up and take control of my life. And once I took hold of the power of choice, I felt unstoppable! I began to take my very first steps in the journey of *truly* enjoying every single day; in addition, the effects of each step rippled into all areas of my life.

The first night after our meeting, I changed my usual routine of putting Drew to bed. Instead of sitting at the foot of his bed and praying fervently that he would be healed, I shifted my perspective and began to pray for myself: that God would help me handle the situation better, that I would find creative ways to incorporate my other kids into Drew's therapy and that I would be able to balance the needs of *all* my children. I prayed that God would strengthen my marriage and help me to become more sensitive to Dan's needs. And finally, I prayed that God would help me to notice the good things that were happening with Drew.

I have to admit, I was surprised at how much better I felt just the very next day, and I know Dan breathed a great sigh of relief as he began to see his wife was coming back to life! That morning, rather than focusing on all the things Drew could not do, like I had in the past, I decided to look for any improvements he *had* been making. I was thrilled to see so many. How he actually looked at me for a few moments, how he responded to his name, how he put his own shoes on, or how he hadn't yet thrown a serious tantrum that day. *Had these little achievements been there all along? I wondered. How had I not noticed them?*

I realized that because I'd been so dialed in to my negative point of view, I'd actually been robbing myself of experiencing all these moments of victory with him. I'd totally been missing the wonderful progress he was making from day to day. Simply by choosing to search for the positive in every challenge with Drew, I began to learn that it was possible to enjoy each day with him...no matter how the autism manifested itself. And as a mom, there is no greater satisfaction than seeing your child succeed! With just a switch of an attitude, I was once again able to engage with my son in this way. The cloud of depression lifted from our household and balance was restored. All because of a sincere choice to see things through a positive viewpoint instead of a negative one, and to enjoy every moment, no matter what that moment might bring.

Now, I'm not going to lie to you; choosing to see the positive in negative situations isn't the easiest thing to do. And pressing forward to enjoy each day even when the world seems to have come against you can be challenging. But it is possible, and if I can do it, you *can* do it. The rewards of the peace and joy that accompany this choice are well worth the struggle, and very soon you'll begin to see every realm of your life begin to transform.

I never dreamed that making this one internal shift in perspective would begin to help me greater enjoy other areas of my life as well, but it did. In the first chapter, I shared how my journey as a weightlifter to the 2008 Olympics was anything but quick and easy. Earlier in my career, I had been plagued not only by injuries, but also significant failures during competitions. In the gym, I'd unofficially be breaking world records but on the competition platforms, images of these former failures haunted my mind and I'd totally bomb out. It was extremely frustrating to be such an under-performer, and I didn't know how I would ever be able to mentally and physically move past those memories of defeat.

In July of 2005, Dan and I had rallied (despite all the turmoil with Drew) and had decided I should begin training again for competition. The only problem was that I was progressing terribly. I couldn't stop thinking about how strong I used to be, how far I had to go to meet competition standards, and even if I did, how would I keep myself from bombing out on the platform? Also at this time, I had a back injury I was attempting to train through, so on top of all the emotional pain I was feeling for Drew, there were days when the physical pain in my body was tremendous.

Three months later after that December meeting with the bishop, however, my performance in the gym was transformed. I had made a firm choice to enjoy each day, no matter what, and this positive mindset affected my training as well. Instead of dreading my workouts, I decided that regardless of how I performed that day, I was going to enjoy every moment of it and train as if it was my last day ever to do so. I let go of my thoughts about where I used to be as a lifter and focused only on the positive aspects of each and every moment of training. Sure enough, as my mental 'muscle' grew stronger by exercising its positive perspective, my body fell in line and did the same. It was like magic! With every workout, I could see a little success, and those little successes each day turned into larger successes each week. By March (only three months later), I had improved by 30kgs (66lbs), a huge gain! I qualified for the National team, and I was setting the tone for the rest of my comeback.

It dawned on me that the reason I had so frequently under-performed in competition earlier in my career was simply because of my negative perspective. While my body had been totally prepared to perform like a champion, my mind would wimp out on the platform. Instead of staying in the moment, enjoying the journey, and thinking "I can do this," my mind would be thinking over and over "I hope I don't bomb out, I hope I don't bomb out..." And consequently, I was a self-fulfilling prophecy; and I'd totally bomb out. Now with my new weapon of positive perspective, I couldn't wait to get out there again and show my coach, myself, and everyone else the kind of champion I really was.

The "Enjoying the Journey" choice continued to spread into every aspect of my life, and simply because of a shift in perspective, I experienced improvement in all realms: my attitude, my family life, my relationships, my business, and my weightlifting.

As I write this book, it's been many years since this transformation has happened in my heart and mind. While I haven't 'arrived' at a place of perfection with regards to enjoying every step of my life journey, I have never regretted making the choice to value and savor every moment of my life. This discipline has helped me walk through the difficult adversities that have arisen, as well as helping me to find a deeper sense of fulfillment and well-being in my life. And I know you want this for your life, too, because you're holding this book in your hands! My desire is to coach you through your own personal choice to enjoy every day of your life, *and* to give you some very practical steps on how to sustain that choice over the course of your entire life. In just a few pages, I'll share those hints with you, but first, let's unpack this concept a bit more.

WHAT ENJOYING THE JOURNEY IS NOT

One very important aspect of enjoying the journey of your life is to understand that when I write "enjoying," I am, by no means, intending this to be interpreted as *ignoring* your realities and simply putting on a happy face. None of us will ever experience true satisfaction or joy in our lives by sticking our heads in the sand and pretending that our problems don't actually exist. At least not long-term satisfaction, anyway. That type of happiness is a facade, and will only wind up adding even more problems and stress to our situations.

As you will read in this book, both Dan and I have walked through some pretty tough adversities, and there have definitely been times when one (or both) of us wanted to put blinders on and act as if the issue was not there. Before Drew was officially diagnosed with autism, I *definitely* wanted to avoid any consultation that would prove my baby to be anything less than perfectly normal. But even in my denial, I could not truly enjoy my life or my family; I only felt the discontentment one feels when they know deep down that they are running from the truth. We knew it was essential that we face our difficulties head-on, deal with the full reality of our situation, and then make the decision to love our lives *anyway*, warts and all.

Maybe you've come to the place where your finances have gone upside down and your debt has spiraled out of control. This is a tough spot to find yourself in, especially if the circumstances that brought you to this point were beyond your ability to prevent. You cannot ignore the realities of that issue, because by doing so, you'll only make the problem bigger and harder to recover from. Both Dan and I have watched as friends have hit roadblocks in the financial realm, and rather than asking for help or making modifications to their lifestyles, they've decided to avoid dealing with it and chose to "enjoy" their lives anyway. But in truth, they only made their state of affairs worse, and eventually lost their businesses, their possessions, and sometimes even their homes. To truly enjoy the journey of life, you've got to reach out for financial wisdom, and step-by-step move toward victory in this area.

Perhaps there's a relationship in your life that is in turmoil, a family member or a spouse. While it might seem at first, so much easier to pretend the conflict doesn't exist, sooner or later, the emotions and pain will resurface. Trying to sweep the situation under the carpet of our hearts is as futile as changing a baby's dirty diaper simply by putting a brand new one on top of the poopy one! It just doesn't work, and we certainly cannot truly enjoy our lives when we are haunted by the discord of loved ones.

Or maybe you've just been given a negative diagnosis from a doctor about your health or the health of a loved one. That sort of news is never easy to reconcile. But the fact is, it's only by looking directly into the truth of the matter that you'll be able to move forward into treatment, and hopefully, a longer and healthier life.

Another clarification I must make is that enjoying the journey of your life does not mean indulging in every sensory desire that happens to pass through your mind. That's just called "no self-restraint." Many people want to "enjoy" their lives by smoking cigarettes, or frequenting the pizza and fast food joints, or never working out and always relaxing in front of the television, but we all know that eventually, these habits will catch up to them. Enjoying the journey of our lives doesn't mean giving in to each of our worldly temptations and disregarding the inevitable circumstances. Rather, it means looking at life squarely in the face and learning to find the best possible moments in each and every day as we strive to be the best person we can possibly be.

Because I know, only too well, how difficult of a habit this can be to form in your everyday routine (especially when you are facing great adversity), I want to offer you four essential keys to help you learn to enjoy the journey of your life. Consider these tips as little exercises to perform each day. I promise you, if you'll be diligent to keep these four keys in the forefront of your mind, your entire perspective upon life will begin to change. Your doubts and fears will be eclipsed by hope and inner strength. I encourage you to write these four tips down on sticky notes and position them in places you see often throughout the day: your bathroom mirror, the dashboard of your car, or the refrigerator. Or maybe even the nightstand next to your bed so that you can begin and end your day thinking of these four essential keys to enjoying the journey of your life.

ONE: FIND JOY

Sometimes when we are in the thick of the dark valleys of life we can convince ourselves that there is absolutely nothing to be happy about, and there exists no reason whatsoever to put a smile on our faces. I get this. I've been there. I know what it feels like to have the weight of depression and defeat so strongly pressing down that it seems as if I would suffocate under it. If you are experiencing this kind of sorrow right now, please understand that I can totally relate with you, and I certainly don't want you to think I'm flippantly trying to convince you to "just choose to be happy." Many times, it's not that easy. But "not easy" does not mean "impossible."

There are times in life when you simply have to fight for it. You've got to want it and you've got to seriously *fight* to find the joy that is available to you each and every day. For me, the hardest time to find joy is in the middle of the night. Because of the autism, Drew does not sleep well so he typically wakes up every morning between 3am and 4am, and he cannot simply be left alone; he must be supervised. When I hear the sound of his waking, I quickly get out of bed so that Dan can sleep. Many times I feel terrible and nauseated from getting up so early, and *every* time, I'm utterly exhausted.

The moment my eyes open, I have a choice: I can hate it and be up all night feeling sick and tired, or I can embrace it, wake up fully, eat some food, and use the time to work on a project. I'm not going to lie to you; there have been a few times when I've picked the former of the two... and I've paid a very grumpy price for it, too. And so did my husband and kids! Consequently, I usually choose the latter and determine to make the best out of an undesirable situation...and there's never been a time that I've regretted that choice.

On the particularly hard days when finding joy seems out of my grasp, I strain my eyes to search more diligently for the good. *What? Drew just ripped off the entire back of my brand new couch and then he threw his older brother's DS out the window?!* (*deep sigh*) As I'm picking up the pieces, I choose to remember that furniture and video games are replaceable; my son is not. Thank Goodness he isn't in a wheelchair, he doesn't need 24-hour professional assistance, and he doesn't have a terminal disease. I remind myself that Dan and I have an amazing marriage, and we are blessed with five wonderful children. It doesn't take long to outshine the bad with thankful thoughts of the good. It's all about perspective.

TWO: SAVOR LIFE

The secret to learning how to savor life is to treat every day like it was your last. Ask yourself: How would I go about this day if I knew it was my last to spend with my spouse, my kids, or even just to do the things I love to do? If this were the case would the landscape of the next 24 hours change at all? Would I treat people differently? Would I waste even a moment of my last day on earth?

Most of us glide through our days on auto-pilot: wake up, get everyone ready and out of the door, work, pick up kids, eat dinner, relax for a bit, then go to bed. Repeat. Repeat again. And again. But what if, even if this routine never varied much, each of us would savor every moment of every day, as if it was the last time we'd ever get to experience it? I guarantee you, even those tasks that just yesterday you called mundane would suddenly come to life and be filled with vibrancy.

Another key to savoring life is to learn to laugh...a lot... every day. We've all heard the famous maxim, "Laughter is the best medicine," and there exist copious amounts of medical and psychological research to prove the truth of this statement. A simple Google search unearths millions of articles about how laughter reduces stress, boosts the immune system, triggers endorphins to flow, and can even relieve pain and protect the heart!

My husband Dan has a great sense of humor (although he'll tell you it took me a while to appreciate it), and even in the midst of chaos, he is ever ready to lighten the mood. He leads our entire family by his example of not getting too serious about the very serious issues we can face at any given time; with Drew, with our busy schedules, and with seven people living under the same roof! This atmosphere of laughter tremendously helps all of us savor each day, even when circumstances seem to be working against us.

Instead of getting frustrated, choose to laugh instead. Rather than letting your anger get the most of you, just count to ten and laugh it off. When you feel the stress starting to rise, ask yourself if the issue *really* is going to matter in the big scheme of things, and try to manage at least a chuckle. You'll be so happy you did.

THREE: LIVE IN THE MOMENT

Living in the moment and savoring life go hand in hand. You cannot live in the moment if you're not good at savoring the moment, and vice versa. This crucial element to enjoying the journey was probably the hardest one for me to incorporate into my everyday life, and even today, I still have to remind myself on a regular basis to slow down, to focus, and to live in the present.

We have no control over the past; what's done is done, and regardless of the consequences, there is absolutely nothing we can do to change it. In fact, the only benefit our past can serve us is to learn from it. And the same holds true for the future. We do not have the ability to stick our heads through a rip in the fabric of time and fiddle around with future events. The *only* component of time that is totally in our command is NOW. This moment. This choice. So why do we spend so much of our days fretting what's happened in the past or worrying about the future?

And yet we all do it, especially us moms. We get so excited about when our kids are going to get older, when they'll be able to dress themselves, clean up after themselves, and what they'll be when they are out of the house. Then the moment they're gone, we wish they were little again, and we wish we would've appreciated them more, and we worry if we taught them everything they needed to know. It seems a little silly to read it so plainly in black and white like that, doesn't it? But as a mother of five, I struggle with this at times and I have to make an effort to remember to enjoy every moment with my children. Before I know it, they will be gone.

Whenever I have the opportunity to speak publicly, I definitely take time to stress the importance of living in the moment, as this discipline was the vital key to me succeeding in a weightlifting comeback and making the 2008 Olympic Team. As I described in the first chapter, it was only because I had learned to keep my mind and body focused on each moment, each lift, and each part of the competition *as it was happening* that I was able to go six for six and break personal and national records. So, as I'm speaking, I'll ask the audience: What are you doing right now? Are you listening, or are you thinking about something else? Are you pressing in to learn something, or are you texting a friend? Usually at that point, the room gets really quiet and everyone becomes very focused; consequently, they are able to hear some truths that if applied will help them experience a higher level of success. If only we could make it our habit to embrace each moment with this type of awareness. We'd certainly live with more passion and be filled with greater fulfillment.

Learn from the past. Plan for the future. Live in the moment.

FOUR: HAVE NO REGRETS

Remember how Superman could do anything unless kryptonite was around? As soon as that green crystal came anywhere near this superhero, he'd begin to grow weaker and weaker until he was totally immobilized. This is a perfect visual metaphor for the attitude of regret, and what Merriam-Webster defines as "to feel sad or sorry about (something that you did or did not do)." Regret is the kryptonite for enjoying the journey, and if you allow these feelings to hang around inside your heart and mind, your ability to enjoy the journey of your life will become completely paralyzed.

I purposefully chose "Have No Regrets" as the fourth strategic tip in this chapter because if you will diligently integrate the first three keys into your life, you'll find it rather difficult to maintain regrets. The only problem is, the moment you shift your thinking away from them and instead begin to focus on regrets, it won't be long before you learn that regret trumps the other three! With thoughts like: "I wish I would've..." "If only I wouldn't have..." "I wonder if I could've..." "I think I should have...", our search for joy will become elusive, and we certainly won't be able to savor each day or live in the moment. See what I mean about regret being like kryptonite?

Again, and please take this to heart, you cannot do *anything* about your past except learn from it. Forgive your mistakes, your bad choices, and maybe even your shortcomings. Let the guilt go, leave the offenses behind, and MOVE ON. Remember this does not mean to ignore it; rather, do whatever you need to do to healthily deal with these issues, and then move forward. You have a wonderful life ahead of you, but only if you will look ahead instead of behind and allow the mistakes of your past (and the victories, too, for that matter) to make you a better person today.

The antidote for regret is straightforward. In fact, the people at Nike have built an enormously successful ad campaign on it for years as they've inspired billions to "Just Do It." Eliminating regret in your life is done by following through. Do what you say you're going to do. Let your "yes" mean yes, and your "no" mean no. And when you are following through, do it to the best of your ability because then you cannot look back and wish you'd have done it better. You will have no regrets. It seems so simple, and yet the effects are quite powerful.

In the first chapter, as I was sharing my experience of the 2008 Olympics, I wrote how on the morning of my event, I possessed complete and utter peace. I knew, without a doubt, that during the prior year of training, I had done everything I knew to do to prepare myself physically, mentally and emotionally for the Olympics. I'd followed through to the absolute best of my ability, and all that remained was for me to compete. That morning, I had not a hint of regret, so I was equipped to savor every second, to live in the moment, and no matter how I ranked when all was said and done, I would be confident that I gave it my *all*. Sure enough, in the end, I did, and the 2008 Olympics was one of the most amazing experiences of my life.

Follow through in all realms of your life. Be there for your loved ones. Call or email the person you promised you would. Pray for the friend who needs it. Finish that project with your child. Start that workout routine. Dust off those dreams in your heart and begin to take steps to see them come true. And in your follow through, give it your 100%. Regret will no longer have any room to hang around in your life.

Find Joy. Savor Life. Live in the Moment. Have No Regrets. If you will incorporate these four strategies into the fabric of your daily life, you will not be able to do anything other than to enjoy the journey of your life!

Four:
Fire in the Belly

Celebrating an American Olympic record!

Chapter Four:
FIRE IN THE BELLY

I LOVE TO WATCH YOUNG CHILDREN AT PLAY. They zoom around with each other, dashing from room to room as they pretend play; one minute they're superheroes saving the world from an onslaught of aliens, the next, they're clutching the soccer world championship. Dreaming is easy for kids, isn't it? It just comes natural for them. When you ask them what they want to be when they grow up, they will answer you with full confidence in their desires to become a professional athlete, a movie star, and the President of the United States. All at the same time. They see everything as possible, and every ambition as attainable.

As adults, we smile and nod our heads, all the while quietly reasoning, "Just you wait, kid. Soon you'll grow up, and sure enough, Life will teach you how to reign in those lofty dreams of yours." The reason we think this way is because somewhere along our path to adulthood, something happened to us that helped us lose our natural knack of dreaming. Maybe a parent, a teacher, or a coach told us how foolish we were and how we'd never be able to accomplish our goals. And we, being children, believed them. Or possibly the reason some of us have become dream-challenged is because an unfortunate situation has altered the course of our lives, and now we think it's too late for us to go for our dreams. Or perhaps, for you, you started out on the journey to fulfill your dreams, but the road proved way more difficult than you'd expected, and you gave up along the way. These kinds of situations happen to all of us.

The only problem is that you and I were born to dream exciting dreams, to achieve new goals, and to expect great lives. And not just in our adolescence, but for the entirety of our walk here on earth. As a result, when we stop dreaming new dreams--the very thing we were created to do—we begin to feel disappointed and dissatisfied with our lives, and that attitude is the very antithesis of enjoying the journey!

Let's not be so quick to inform the kids around us of the improbabilities of their dreams. Obviously, it's true that a single person cannot be an athlete, a star, and the president all at once. But what if, instead of us adults feeling the need to teach the children how to curb their desires to fit inside the box of probability, we allowed ourselves to learn from *them* how to dream big, and how to see the impossible as possible? We could exchange with them a little of our maturity for a little of their ingenuity. If you ask me, I'd say we could learn a lot from each other.

Whatever your case may be, let me encourage you: If you are serious about enjoying the journey of your life, then it's time to learn to dream again. It's time to look inside your heart and to determine what unique gifts and qualities you possess, and how you'd like to utilize them to fulfill those dreams. And when I say "dreams," it's important for me to acknowledge that they come in all shapes and sizes. Big dreams, medium-sized dreams, and dreams that will take the rest of your life to accomplish. It might be a hobby, a sport, or a musical instrument you've always wanted to try. It might be a side business you'd think could be fun and could bring in a little extra money for your family. However, for some of you, it may even be a complete career change. (Although before you do anything drastic, like quitting your job, make sure you've read this entire book, especially the chapters on teamwork and goal setting!) No matter what the dreams are that you possess, those dreams are inside of you to be lived out...not to lay dormant on a shelf inside your heart just gathering dust. Keep in mind the words I used to close out the first chapter, "Just pick a dream, and go for it!"

FIRE IN THE BELLY

For some of us, the picking of the dream is easy; it's the "going for it" part where we find ourselves falling short. We just don't seem to have the gumption anymore to step out and try something new. If that is true for you, then this chapter is going to be a catalyst for your dream! I want to help you stir up your energy so you can find the desire within yourself to make your goals and dreams come true. Because the truth is, desire is a crucial component to enjoying the journey of life. If dreams are the vehicles that carry us along that journey, then desire is the fuel that enables our dreams to become reality. And we all know that unless our cars have gas in them, we aren't going to go anywhere. Desire is everything!

There's a term Dan and I refer to when we speak of desire; it's one we learned very early on. "The Fire in the Belly." Years ago, when Dan ran for the Washington State House of Representatives for the first time he was mentored by a great man named Kent Pullen. Not only was Kent a former State Senator and King County Councilman, but he was also a mathematical genius. He had developed a "scoring criteria" for potential candidates that helped qualify their success ratio. This equation scored a person on their: knowledge of the issues, past elected experience, community involvement, general appearance and demeanor, ability to handle stress, ability to raise money, work ethic, speaking dynamic, management skills, and many other criteria.

After explaining the details of his equation, Kent looked Dan in the eyes and said, "But even after all of this, there is one more factor that can trump them *all*, and that's 'the Fire in the Belly'." He went on to clarify what he meant. The fire in the belly is that deep down passion that burns in the core of who you are. It's the white-hot desire that propels a person to strive toward a dream, no matter what the cost. Obi Wan Kenobi called it "The Force." Rocky Balboa's coach called it "The Eye of the Tiger." Kent Pullen called it "The Fire in the Belly," and he told Dan that it would trump experience and talent and perfect resume's and all the rest…every time.

As a 25-year-old young man, straight out of college, with no resume, no experience and little knowledge of the issues, Dan lost his first election to an 'old pro' by less than .5%! The fire in Dan's belly only grew hotter. He came back in two years and handily defeated the incumbent. Yes, he outranked Dan on elected experience, community involvement, work experience, money raised, etc., etc., but Dan still beat him by an unapologetic work ethic and by his fire in the belly.

Some people think that talent and experience are the keys to success, but I have seen many, many extremely talented *and* experienced people never see their dreams fulfilled because they lacked this fire in their belly. They simply did not have the inner desire to make their dreams a reality. Desire not only fuels discipline and determination, but it also keeps a person focused to stay the course until he or she reaches the finish line. Talent can certainly get you in the car, and possibly even spark the engine enough to start, but only desire has the power to carry you through to the end when the journey is painstakingly uphill or when there seems to be too many roadblocks and potholes.

Since the late 90's, Dan and I have owned a business together called Roach Gymnastics. We have over 50 employees, and 1000+ kids come through our doors each month as they have fun learning gymnastics from our high-quality coaches. We offer recreational gymnastics as well as competitive gymnastics, up to Level 10. As I watch our competitive teams mature, I can always tell which girls have the potential to become true champions. While any athlete must have a level of talent for their sport, the quality that shines through the most is their fire in the belly. The girl that gives her 110%, no matter what, is the girl who will eventually rise to the top and win the gold medals. She'll beat out the girl with more talent but less desire every time.

Young or old, we all have a reservoir of desire inside of us waiting to be tapped. Later in this chapter, I'll give you some keys to unlocking the power of desire to make your dreams a reality; but first, let's differentiate what's a dream, and what's just a fantasy.

LEGITIMATE DREAM
OR ROCK-N-ROLL FANTASY?

We've all seen the catastrophes that can happen during the audition phase of the hit show, *American Idol*. The girl who struts into the room full of confidence and begins to totally win over the judges; that is, until she opens her mouth to sing. She starts off out-of-tune, and only continues to get worse as the song crescendos. And then she misses the judges' hands urging her to stop because her eyes are closed as she passionately sings with gusto. One would think the sound of the howling dogs coming in from outside would've given her a clue.

She finishes her song, and opens her eyes, fully expecting a good review from the judges and a ticket to Hollywood. Sadly, she is utterly shocked when the judges tell her she has no real ability to sing. And then, the judges are shocked that she is shocked, not to mention the shock of the millions in the television audience (including myself) who are watching this entire train wreck! When I've seen this, I've thought, *This poor girl. Surely, she's sung for other people before. Haven't any of them loved her enough to tell her the truth? Or maybe, they have, and she just didn't listen.* Either way, this is the case of a person who might have desire, but has chosen to drive her desire down a road that was never meant for her. Although sometimes I cringe from their brutal honesty, I do appreciate how many times the *American Idol* judges try to redirect those misguided kids as they suggest to them other areas they might think about pursuing.

Before you spend too much time, energy and resources going for a dream, you must learn to discern which ideas can honestly be turned into successful endeavors and which are simply fantasy. To do this, you've got to get brutally honest with yourself, *and* allow others to be brutally honest with you. For instance, with this girl above, before she set out for these nationally televised auditions, she should've sought the advice of a mentor or a voice teacher, someone with a sincere knowledge of music. If she would've sung for them, and received their feedback, she could've foregone a public and humiliating rejection on *American Idol*. (Note: When seeking realistic advice, sometimes your mom or your boyfriend cannot be impartial enough. This also goes for someone who has a personal interest in your pursuit, like a music teacher who wants to keep your business.) Whatever your dream is, find someone who has either done what you want to do or has great knowledge in that field. Allow them to speak into your life and help you decipher if your dream is within the realm of possibility, or if it's simply a whim that you lack the skill set to achieve.

Limit your procurement of advice *only* to those who are truly qualified. The fulfillment of your dream cannot be based on a democracy. If Dan and I had gone with the majority of voters when we began to pursue the possibility of me making a comeback for the 2008 Olympics, we'd never have done it. When we first told them, our families thought we were nuts to even consider it! In their defense, I *was* over 30, and all the other competitors would be in their early 20s, I *had* just given birth to our third baby six weeks prior to our discussion...and, oh yeah, I had a bad back with a herniated disc. All of those reasons most certainly made our dream look like a rock-n-roll fantasy.

The first thing we did was discuss the dream with my coach; he was immediately onboard. From there, we promptly went to my chiropractor and carefully counted the costs the physical strain of lifting would have on my back. He believed that if we were strategic in the planning of my comeback, we could definitely have a great chance of success. And then, I had a few other things going for me: I had been on the top before, and I fully understood the physical, mental, and emotional process to get there again. I had always been a gifted athlete, and I still was. And most importantly, I possessed the level of desire needed to make the great sacrifices I knew I would need to make in order to achieve our goal. Yes, my Olympic dream was highly improbable...but impossible? Well, obviously not. We did it!

And no matter how improbable *your* dream is, if you have been realistic in your dream selection, you can do it, too. But you must have the power of desire going for you. Here are three keys to help you tap into your deep internal reservoir of desire.

TURNING DESIRE INTO A DREAM
1. NO EXCUSES

Why is it that for some of us, the first thing our minds do when we set out to accomplish a dream is come up with every reason why our pursuit is doomed to fail? Excuse after excuse rings in our heads. "I'm not good enough to do this." "The last time I tried this, I failed. What makes me think this time will be different?" "I'm way too old to be trying this." "I don't have enough money." "I don't have enough time." "I don't have enough experience." Blah, blah, blah...and before we know it, these excuses not only have extinguished the fire of desire, but also have completely disqualified us from even attempting to go for our dreams.

Hey, I get it. If you want to talk about excuses and disqualifications, I have a string of personal experiences to share with you. In '94, when I was just starting out of the gate as a weightlifter, I had everything going for me, as far as talent was concerned. But I was only 19 years old, my personal life was a wreck, and as a result, I gave up and quit. For over a year, I allowed my excuses to put out the fire of my dreams. Then in '96, I was able to rekindle my desire, and I began to train again. While it's true that over the next two years I soared to the top of the ranks and received international recognition, my success was short-lived as I publicly bombed out at the '98 World Championships, followed by the 1999 Pan American Games where I injured my elbow and didn't place. The year leading up to the Olympics, I had to claw my way back up the ranks to put myself in a position to qualify for the Olympic team. Then, just weeks before the Olympic Trials, I herniated a disc in my back which not only dashed my Olympic dreams, but ended my career. Or so I thought. I had to face the fact that my 2000 Olympic dream was out of my reach. I felt as if I'd been on a terrible rollercoaster ride and I was heart-broken.

In 2002, there were still embers glowing in my belly for my Olympic dream; perhaps I could make the 2004 team? I fanned the flames of desire, and trained like mad. Again, I quickly rose to the top, and it appeared as if this was going to be my chance. However, just as I was within striking distance, the pain from my old back injury returned with a vengeance, taking me out of the running once again. When Dan and I began to consider a comeback for the 2008 Olympics, let me assure you, there were plenty of excuses to douse over the fire of our Olympic dream. The odds were definitely stacked against me!

But more than the list of excuses, there was another thought that haunted me even more, and that thought is what I wrote about at the close of the last chapter. "Have no regrets." The Olympic dream was so big on the inside of me, I knew that if I didn't do everything I could to make that dream come true, I'd regret it for the rest of my life. 2008 would truly be my last year to make a comeback. If I didn't go for it with all my might, would I live the rest of my days wondering, *What if...?* Even if I did everything in my power to make the team and still fell short, at least I would go to the grave knowing I gave my 110%, and I'd have no regrets.

What is the dream that stubbornly keeps poking you on the shoulder to finally turn around and give it full attention? Stop making excuses, light the fire in your belly, and go for your dream. Instead of imagining all the reasons *not* to move forward, project forward in your life for a moment, and begin to imagine how great it will feel to have given your all to make that dream come to pass. Even if, at the end of the day, the result isn't exactly what you'd pictured, knowing that you gave it your 110% to achieve your goal will be substantially more satisfying than the regret of never having tried at all.

2. GET UP!

This one comes as a surprise to many people, but once a goal has been settled upon, we actually have to get up off the couch and do something! Dan and I hire many young people to work and to coach at Roach Gymnastics, and we are constantly amazed at how many teens come onboard as employees and then are shocked that they, in fact, must show up on time *and* work to get their paycheck. Maybe it's an attitude of entitlement; maybe it's apathy; maybe it's simply poor upbringing. Whatever the case, in order to accomplish anything worth accomplishing, it's going to take work. Hard work. And most of the time, lots of it.

Do something today to make your dream closer to a reality. Start taking steps, even if they are little, to move forward. In a later chapter of this book I'm going to offer you detailed steps about how to set goals and to strategize success, but in conjunction with igniting the fire in your belly, there's no better way to fan the flames than to get up off the couch and begin activating your dream. Do you want to lose weight? Then start working out today, even if it's just for 10 minutes. Do you want to start a business? Go to the library and check out books about how to begin. Do you want your marriage to be better? Before you go to bed tonight, sit down with your spouse, look him or her in the eyes, and tell them something you love about them. Ask them out on a date, even if it's a stay-at-home date! Sometimes those are the best kind.

If you will do *something* every day towards accomplishing your dreams, I guarantee that every night when you lay your head on your pillow, you will feel a greater sense of fulfillment and confidence in yourself. You will be learning how to enjoy every day of your life.

3. CELEBRATE EACH VICTORY

The bigger the dream, the longer the journey to accomplish it. As a result, during that journey, we will have more opportunities to become discouraged, to hit roadblocks, to become fatigued, and to lose our desire for the dream. One way to combat this is to take the time to celebrate every little victory along the way. Sometimes we can become so focused on accomplishing the long-term goal, we can neglect the victory of each step it takes to get there. Unfortunately, when we forget to pat ourselves on the back, we will also find our desire and energy beginning to wane.

When I began training for my 2008 Olympic comeback, those first weeks were daunting for me. The amount I was lifting was so far from what I knew I'd eventually need to be lifting in order to qualify for the team. It was overwhelming to think about how I'd possibly be able to hit those amounts of weight. However, instead of allowing the end goal to loom intangibly in the distance, I chose to live in the moment, and to enjoy each step of the way. That meant setting small daily, weekly, and monthly goals for myself and then having my own little celebration each time I hit one of them! Sure enough, the small victories turned into big victories, and before I knew it, I was on a plane en route to Beijing!

You were born to dream, *and* you were given everything you need on the inside to accomplish your dreams. If you're finding you've become a bit rusty in the dreaming department, spend an afternoon watching a group of children playing at the park. Allow them to help you remember your own youthful days of believing in the impossible. Then look inside to whatever it is that you know you've always wanted to try or to achieve. Assess that dream with brutal honesty. After you've focused your vision to see exactly what you'd love to do...Fan the Fire in Your Belly and Go For It! Silence the excuses, get up off the couch of life, and celebrate your victories all the way to your finish line.

Five:
You Gotta Have A Plan

*I started with my ultimate goal, the 2008 Olympics,
and worked backwards.*

Chapter Five:
YOU GOTTA HAVE A PLAN

WE COULD HARDLY WAIT TO GET THERE. It was the Fall of 2008, just a few months after the Olympics, and our family was going on our first vacation in four years. The cold, rainy days of the Pacific Northwest had settled in, so what better place to visit than sunny and tropical Hawaii? Dan, myself, and our three children (ages 7, 5, and 3) were buckled in and ready for take-off with our carry-ons properly stowed, our electronic devices turned off, and our seat backs and tray tables locked in their upward positions. Our goal for this trip was simple: relaxation. Beyond that, we really didn't have a plan.

The first couple days on The Island passed without a hitch. Of course, looking back, I recognize that even for a family of five, there really isn't a large margin for error when the schedule for the day is: wake up, eat, swim, relax, eat, swim, relax, eat, relax, sleep. By Day 3, Dan and I got the idea that it would be a bummer for the entire family to have flown all the way out here and to not have taken advantage of touring Pearl Harbor. What a fun, spontaneous thing to do! So we packed everybody up, asked the concierge for directions, and set out toward Pearl Harbor.

As soon as we pulled into the historic site, I thought that perhaps we should've asked the concierge more questions about the optimum time to take this field trip because it looked like we arrived just moments *after* everyone else (i.e., hundreds of people). Not only did we have to park out in the back-40 somewhere and walk a half-mile to get to the entrance, but also we had to wait a very long time in the admission line. In the hot, Hawaiian sun. With three small children. And one of them was already starting to do the "potty dance."

Once we got inside the facility, we had to stand in another long line to get the tickets for the ferryboat that took the tourists out into the harbor. Now, I really started to wonder if we should've formulized a bit more of a plan for this outing, but I tried to stay positive. Finally, we arrived at the front of the line...only to find out there were no bathrooms on the ferryboat. For another family, this might not have been a huge deal, but for us, this was not the case. With our youngest daughter just potty-trained and our 5-year-old autistic son who couldn't communicate and would literally pull down his pants to go if he couldn't find a bathroom, a lavatory-free ferryboat was a deal-breaker. So we all had to turn around and take the short hike back to the car without ever being able to enjoy Pearl Harbor.

Dan and I were so disappointed, and the kids were not happy that almost a full day of their "eat, swim, relax, eat, swim, relax" schedule had been swallowed up by long lines and even longer car rides. As we drove back to our hotel, Dan and I talked about how frustrating it was that after all the work we had exerted to visit Pearl Harbor, in the end, we had to leave without being able to experience what we came for. And it was all because we had done a poor job of planning. If only we had asked more questions and done a bit more research about what exactly we would be encountering, we could've made a more accurate plan about how to successfully accomplish a trip to Pearl Harbor.

Probably all of us, as we've journeyed through the path of life, have experienced this type of scenario. We find ourselves disappointed with the way a particular goal or event has panned out, but when we stop to analyze the issue, we realize that the result was simply a manifestation of our lack of planning. From small goals to big goals, I believe much of what we label as "failure," really could've been prevented if only we'd have done a better job on the front end of the situation. A wise and well-thought out plan can be the deciding factor of whether you will succeed or fail (and by "fail," I mean, "give up before you've tried until you've succeeded.")

Every endeavor is easier and more productive when you have taken the time to map out a plan about how to get from Point A to Point B! I often wonder how many people are not enjoying the journey of their lives simply because they have dreams and visions of where they want to go, but no roadmap to help them arrive at the destinations of their goals. A dream without a plan of action will only bring feelings of frustration and discontentment. Or maybe, for some, you have put together a plan of attack, but it's too vague, or unrealistic, or it has become out-of-date.

Other than the Pearl Harbor debacle, when I'm thinking about attempting anything, big or small, I tend to swing way over to the other side of the non-planning pendulum (sometimes to my husband's chagrin), because I love to strategize a plan. And once I see that plan completed on paper, I like to re-strategize the strategy of my carefully strategized plan. (Can anyone say, "Type-A Personality"?!) If you are not naturally bent this way, I am so glad you have this book in your hands. My desire is to help you learn some very practical ways to set the goals you need to achieve in order to transform your dream into a reality. In fact, the information in these next pages will be feasible enough for you to build a concrete, detailed plan of action, so you might find it worthwhile to have a pen and pad of paper readily available.

The first, and most obvious...

Action Step #1:
Identify the Specific Goal

"Specific" is the operative word, here. It is not enough to say, "I'd really like to be a successful business owner," but have no idea of exactly what kind of business you desire to launch. Dreams that are formless and hazy like this are probably just fantasies (like we talked about in Chapter Four). For instance, at the time of writing this book, Dan and I are the proud parents of five children. If we decided to take our family on a motor-home vacation from Seattle to California, it will do us no good if our destination is simply "California." I don't even want to think about trying to plan and pack for our family of seven to take a road trip to the huge state of California without a very specific end location. That would be a nightmare! However, if our destination is Disney Land in Anaheim, California; that's a completely different story. Now I would be able to know exactly how many days it will take to get there, how much food to prepare, how many clothes to pack, how many movies to bring for the portable DVD player, etc. Sure, it will still be a great deal of work to prepare for the trip, but at least I'd be able to rest assured that I was on the right track and my efforts were accurately focused.

It's the same way with whatever dream you hold in your heart. Before you can set forth a workable plan to reach your goal, you must be able to specify exactly what it is you want to achieve. For me, one of the biggest dreams I've accomplished to date was making the 2008 Olympic Team. In this chapter, as we walk through the steps about how to formulate a plan, I will use this experience to exemplify how I personally applied these steps. The Olympic strategy is an ideal example to use because my time frames and goal markers needed to be extremely specific, but this template for goal setting has worked even for other situations in my life when the end-goals were less cut-and-dried and didn't possess mandatory time frames.

When Dan and I sat down in 2005 to set forth a tangible strategy for my weightlifting career, the goal was crystal clear: Make the 2008 Olympic Team. It was very specific. It wasn't "Train extra diligently and see how close to the Olympics I could get." It wasn't "Focus on weightlifting and maybe make the Olympic Team, or if nothing else, compete in other competitions." No. Our goal was intentional and exact: Make the 2008 Olympic Team.

When you are identifying your goal, try to be as specific as possible. Instead of writing down, "My goal is to lose weight," write, "My goal is to lose XX lbs. in XX months." Can you see how much more deliberately you can plan with the latter example? Instead of writing down, "My goal is to start a sewing business," write, "My goal is to launch a part-time alterations service in the city of XX." Again, the second one will generate more distinct strategies. Instead of "My goal is to complete my college education," write, "My goal is to complete my college degree, majoring in XX, by the year XX."

Take the time to think about the precise goal at hand. If you find you are unable to get this specific, perhaps you should spend more time evaluating if this goal is the right one for you, or if you truly are ready to embark on the journey. It's better to prepare yourself more fully and to be able to start with confidence, than to jump in unprepared and consequently be forced to prematurely abort the ship of your dream.

Once you've Identified your Specific Goal...

Action Step #2:
Brainstorm!

This is the fun part. Begin brainstorming all the possible ways you could make it to your end result. Brainstorm a list of things that must happen in order for you to get started. Identify what your needs are. What kind of capital will your goal require? Will you need any staff when you begin? Will you need particular training to achieve your goal? Make Google your best friend and research, research, research.

Once you have brainstormed all the possible strategies and everything you think you might need, meet with someone who is an expert in your field or with someone who has successfully accomplished a goal similar to yours. Ask them to look at your list and to offer advice about how to improve it. And then brainstorm some more.

For our Olympic goal, Dan and I came up with a list of things we knew were vital. We formulated a financial plan for the next few years. Aware of the incredible time commitment that Olympic training requires, we devised a daily, weekly and monthly schedule for our family. This exposed how important outside help with the kids would be, so we then came up with a plan about who to ask. We knew we would need help running Roach Gymnastics, so we set out to hire a new manager. Then, to maximize time, focus and effort, we asked Coach Thrush if he would move his training facility into our Roach Gymnastics building. This was a complete Win/Win for all of us. For me, I could not only train there daily, but I could also keep an eye on the day-to-day production of our business. For Coach Thrush, we were able to give his facility more visibility and help him grow his business. Do you see how intentional and creative both Dan and I became? By combining resources, we were able to take a nearly impossible goal and tangibly turn it toward the possible.

Sometimes once you begin putting everything on paper, you can feel overwhelmed by all that is needed and become tempted to give up even before you've gotten started. Don't throw in the towel so soon! Keep brainstorming until you've devised a viable solution.

Action Step #3:
Go to the End, and Work Your Way Backwards

I remember sitting down with Dan along with copious amounts of paper and markers, calculating how much time we had until the Olympics. I made a time line by writing down the competitions in reverse order. I knew that at the Olympic Trials in 2008, I would need to be in the top four, so by the end of 2007, I needed to be in the top 5 or 6, et cetera, et cetera. I worked my way back, all the way to the beginning (of me sitting that night at my table compiling this list), and figured out what my workout goals needed to be each week and month in order to attain these goal markers.

I made a list of every female competitor who, at the time of my planning, was ranked ahead of me, and researched to find out exactly how much I needed to lift in order to pass them by and move up in the ranks. I did this both with American weightlifters in my weight class, and with international lifters in my weight class. You see,

I knew I wasn't going to become #1 overnight. The girls I was competing against were 10+ years younger than me, and none of them were raising three small children, running a business, and dealing with the effects of autism. My journey to the top was going to be a slow process.

Most significant achievements are accomplished by a long passage of discipline and hard work. It almost always takes longer to "get there" than what we wanted. This is why it's so important, as you work your way backwards to set attainable small goals along the way. Be generous with yourself and set yourself up to succeed by creating the shorter-term milestones ones that are realistic for you to reach. If, as you look at your time line, you realize that even the smaller milestones you will need to achieve in order to reach your end goal are simply going to be unattainable, then perhaps you need to renegotiate your time line. Maybe this goal will take longer than you originally thought it would.

For me, with the 2008 Olympics, we had a set end-date that was non-negotiable. By the Olympic Trials, I had to be at the physical capacity to qualify for the team. The end. If, as Dan and I were working backwards and setting smaller goals we would've come to realize that I just was not going to be able to hit the needed mile-markers in the time-frame allotted, we would've had to reevaluate if our Olympic dream was going to be worth the vast amounts of time and effort we'd need to spend. But for most people going for dreams outside the athletic arena, end-dates can be a bit more flexible. Don't give up your goal just because you realize it's going to take longer to reach it. Keep the dream alive by simply expanding your timeline a bit. Enjoying the journey isn't about achieving all your dreams and getting to the end as fast as possible, right? It's about enjoying every day as we journey through our lives.

Action Step #4:
Begin! Take it Step-by-Step, Goal-by-Goal.

I know I'm stating the obvious, but once you have a plan in place, you actually need to start! I've known people who spend all their time in Steps 1-3, repeating them over and over, and never actually move past the planning stage into the action stage. They have fooled themselves into thinking that all the energy they are exerting in the visionary/planning stage is in fact propelling them forward toward their end goal. What's really happening is they are procrastinating getting up from the drawing board and stepping out into the hard work of their dream. Don't fall into this trap. Assemble your plan of attack carefully...and then, Attack!

And take it goal by goal. I believe the biggest reason people fail is because they are faithful to set the long-term goal, but forget to set the thousands of short-term goals necessary to get there. To be successful, you have to bring your best to every day and hit your goals...every day. For me this meant I needed a nap every day because without a nap, I wouldn't be one hundred percent during my workout. I needed to take an ice bath every day because if I didn't ice, I wouldn't recover as quickly. I had a very strict diet that I adhered to each day because if I didn't eat right, it would affect my training. The only problem was, I would've loved to skip my naps because that would've given me more hours in my day to accomplish things, and I would've really enjoyed eating some of the less-nutritious foods the rest of my family was eating. Oh yeah...and I hate cold water! But I knew if I was not willing to stay diligent with the little goals then I could forget about my big, Olympic goal, because I never was going to get there.

While it's important to keep your ultimate goal in your mind's eye, most of your energies from day-to-day need to be focused on succeeding step-by-step and goal-by-goal. It's not bad to want to be #1, but you need to start at wherever you are today and methodically move up in the ranks. Because if daily your primary focus is on becoming #1, or achieving your ultimate goal, then even when you hit your smaller milestones, you will not feel a sense of accomplishment. You'll grow discouraged and most likely give up. Keep "#1" — or whatever that means in your case — in its proper place. Use that visual from time to time to remind yourself of why you are working like crazy every day, but don't allow it to overshadow the smaller, less impressive goals you need to meet before you get there. Use the main goal as motivation, but focus on the day to day.

When we embarked on our Olympic dream, I was nowhere near being #1, but I had learned that I could not allow that reality to distract me. I remember saying after the 2006 Nationals, "It doesn't matter where I'm ranked right now, its in 2008 that matters." Sure it was humbling to get out there, to compete and to not be on top, but I could not afford to get off track from the process. I knew my focus needed to be on doing everything I could from day-to-day in order to position myself for where I wanted to be down the road. And sure enough, by the time the 2008 Olympics had rolled around, I went to Beijing ranked #1 on our American Olympic team.

You can do it. You can reach your ultimate goal if you will diligently do the work along the way. NOTE: It's the day-to-day, unglorified work in the trenches where champions are formed.

Action Step #5:
Celebrate Each Victory!

I already talked about this in Chapter 4, but I must take a few sentences to reiterate how crucial this is. Every time you hit one of your smaller milestones, reward yourself! Stop for a moment and congratulate yourself for the hard work you are exerting. Reflect upon where you were when you started and notice the progress you've made. So often, as soon as we hit a goal, we immediately set out to hit the next one without so much as a thought about what it was we just accomplished.

Stopping for a bit and celebrating each victory will refuel your motivation and continue to build your confidence that your ultimate goal is within your reach. Just like a car, if you never stop to refuel, you'll start to peter out and lose the energy it will take to press toward the final goal.

TROUBLESHOOTING YOUR PLAN

So you have your beautifully structured plan, all color-coded and organized. You've laminated the timeline and posted it where everyone can see it. You stand back to gaze at it, and comment about how brilliantly perfect is your plan.

And then you get started. And then you hit roadblocks and all sorts of unexpected twists and turns. And then you want to throw the entirety of your artistically-crafted, color-coded, and perfectly laminated plan in the trash!

Trust me, I completely understand because I've been there many, many times. I've had to learn that I cannot become a slave to the original schedule, and that inevitably, something is bound to happen that was not part of my plan. I had to be flexible when after we set out to achieve an Olympic dream, my 2½-year-old son was diagnosed with autism. Then again, I had to re-analyze the plans when less than a year before the Olympics, I found myself needing back surgery. Sometimes major roadblocks like these will threaten your dreams, and you will need to re-evaluate, re-structure, and re-formulate your plan of attack. And I'm not going to lie to you; sometimes these situations will detour you completely from your original goals, and you will be left with a choice: wallow in disappointment or pick yourself up, embrace it, and move on.

Learn to be fluid with your plan of attack, and perhaps forego the laminator. Instead, use pencils and paper or dry-erase markers and white boards. If you will expect the unexpected, then you won't be shocked when events don't go as planned. You'll be able to adapt quickly, to learn from your mistakes, to reorganize a new strategy, and consequently, to never lose faith in your ultimate goal.

Never underestimate the power of a well-thought-out plan! If you are finding it difficult right now to enjoy the journey of your life, ask yourself if it's because you have dreams and visions of where you want to be going, but have forgotten to strategize the roadmap to arrive at the destination of your goal. Remember, a dream without a plan of action will only bring feelings of frustration and discontentment. Set out today to begin formulating a plan of action. Set your goal, brainstorm your line of attack, determine your mile markers along the way, and then... get to it!

Let the Dreams Begin!

Six:
It Takes a Village

My Village: my extended family; my back surgeon,
Dr. Robert Bray; my chiropractor, Dr. Greg Summers;
Coach John Thrush; my husband, Dan; and my teammates.

Chapter Six:
IT TAKES A VILLAGE

THERE IS AN ANCIENT AFRICAN PROVERB, "It takes a village to raise a child." This adage was made popular in our nation by a book written by former First Lady Hillary Clinton, but many people don't realize its origin came from Africa. And not just one African tribe held this proverb as a standard for their subculture; for thousands of years, many tribes throughout the entire continent, and in their unique languages and dialects, have passed this wisdom down from generation to generation. The wordage differs slightly from account to account, but the general idea remains consistent: In order to accomplish something as significant as raising a healthy child, parents will need the help of those around them. In other words; it's going to take teamwork.

This proverb holds true for just about any important undertaking. If the dream you are going for is important and noteworthy, like building a successful marriage and family, or starting a business, or overcoming an addiction, or transforming your life habits from unhealthy to healthy, while you might be able to accomplish it all by yourself, it will be much easier if you have a team around you to help. When you attempt to go solo, there is no one to motivate you forward when the going gets rough and everything inside you wants to quit. When you are by yourself, there is no one present to help you strategize your game plan or answer the questions you don't have answers for. And when you are all alone, the joys of successes are left unshared and the burdens of your mistakes feel very heavy.

I think I can go as far as to say that if any of us wants to enjoy the journey of our life, we're going to need a village to do it! It's going to take the relationships, the support, the encouragement, and sometimes the resources of your spouse, your family, your friends, and constituents. And in my case, I knew it was going to take a village to raise an Olympic athlete.

But first, before I talk about the value of teamwork, I owe you a full personal disclosure. You see, asking for help is not exactly one of my core strengths. I'm a focused, driven person, who even as a young teen, loved the challenge of setting lofty goals and working my hardest to make them come to pass, even when I lacked the support of those around me. I learned to become quite self-sufficient, and to this day, find tremendous satisfaction in completing a job well done. And if that was not enough, I also can have perfectionist tendencies. "If you want it done right, you have to do it yourself, right?" Needless to say, my A-type personality has never been easily bent towards reaching out to others for help unless I'd already tried everything in my own power to accomplish the task at hand.

Chances are, if you are anything like me, you know exactly where I'm coming from...which is why I'm dedicating an entire chapter to the incredible value of teamwork. Dan has been a great role model for me in this area because as an elected official who has run numerous election campaigns, he fully understands how critical a strong support system is for success. By following his example throughout the years, I have learned not only how to ask for help, but also what types of people to ask to help, and how to keep the members of the team motivated and satisfied.

CRUCIAL TEAM MEMBERS

There are two very important team members whom, I believe, must be on board with any dream or any goal. Moving forward in the journey of life without both of these two vital influencers is a non-negotiable. They are, first and foremost, God, and secondly, your spouse.

When I am considering any major undertaking, without fail, I make sure to consult the Lord. I know that perfect wisdom can only come from Him, and so I check in with Him to make sure I'm going in the right direction. In addition, I am gravely aware that I cannot accomplish anything significant unless it is through His strength working on the inside of me.

Every decision Dan and I make in regards to life goals, family goals, or career goals, we approach through prayer. I check in with my gut feeling, and if I feel it's not the right thing to pursue, or not the best decision to make, I pay attention to that feeling, and I don't do it. On the other hand, when I feel good and at peace about the direction I'm taking, I go for it and give it everything I've got. It's so important to ponder and think about the steps in front of you before you actually jump into them. Don't be in such a hurry that you ignore or simply do not recognize what your gut is telling you...Wait! Be in tune with the Lord, and allow His peace in your heart to guide your steps.

And secondly, I want to stress as strongly as I can without writing this in all-caps, your spouse must be in agreement with the goal you desire to pursue. I firmly believe that the single most important and influential person in anyone's life is his or her spouse; therefore, it is vital that the spouse play an active roll in the journey of your dream. It's not enough for the partner to say, "I support you, honey. You go do your thing as long as it doesn't interfere with what I'm doing." This kind of attitude will not last long, especially if the dream is time consuming, and in the end, there will be resentment from both parties.

If you are pursuing something big, and your spouse is not in total support of it, I do not recommend the pursuit, because the more time and effort involved in the goal, the more time and distance that will come between you and your spouse. Before you know it, you'll be strangers, resentful and lacking. What is the point of you running off to chase your dream only to turn around after the fact and find your family in shambles? Think about it. Is your success really worth this price? Don't sacrifice your marriage on the altar of your dream. No matter how much you accomplish, when the adrenaline fades, you'll find yourself in regret.

Both Dan and I are big dreamers, and we have learned to support each other in those goals and never allow one's pursuit to eclipse the others'. In fact, if you looked at a time graph of our marriage up to this point, you'd be able to clearly see how often we've traded off. One season, we are chasing an Olympic dream for me, and the next, we are chasing a political dream for him. And then there are times when we are both pursuing the same goals, like building a business or raising our kids. We make sure to stay in tandem as we make everything a joint effort.

If you are married, you simply cannot fully enjoy the journey of life if your relationship with your spouse is strained. I'd recommend that you set your present goal aside and change your dream to improving your marriage. Only when that foundation is strong and secure would I move on to other dreams and desires. Here are some practical ways to strengthen your marriage and family:

• Make time every day to discuss things like child rearing, business decisions, finances, schedules, etc. Always be checking in with each other to keep the lines of communication open.

• Try to date 3-4 times a month. If you have kids, this means time spent away from them! It doesn't have to be expensive, but it does need to be fun. NOTE: a date is not the time to discuss the items from above. This is a time for you and your spouse to reconnect, to dream together, to simply be together.

• If you have kids, try making one evening a week "family night." Play together, go for a walk together, and occasionally, watch a fun movie together.

• Go to church. Aside from the obvious reason of strengthening your relationship with God, faithfully attending a church is an amazing way to build relationships with other married couples, for your kids to make great friends, and for you to build a strong support system for your entire family. Dan and I are members of the Church of Jesus Christ of Latter Day Saints, or "Mormons" and we love the structure, the faith, the love, and the support our church family provides. Church can help make your family stronger and better.

CHOOSE WISELY

Once Dan and I had made the firm decision to aggressively pursue my comeback for the 2008 Olympics, the first thing we did was to strategize our team. With his political career, with our flourishing business, Roach Gymnastics, with our three children under 4 years of age, and with the all-consuming task of training for the Olympics, we knew without a doubt the only way success would be possible was for us to carefully organize a team of people. It is very important to add here that Dan and my snapshot of "success" was not merely one of me competing in the 2008 Olympics. That was only a portion of the picture. Our vision of success was for me to make the Olympic team and for us to still have maintained a strong marriage, family and business. If we would have accomplished the Olympics at the cost of our relationship with each other, or with our children and close friends, we would not have deemed the journey "successful" at all. No accomplishment or promotion is worth that dear price.

Dan and I were painstakingly cautious when choosing the members of what we soon called, "Team Roach." We knew the people we picked were going to be crucial in our Olympic journey, and would, in fact, make or break our chances of success. First, we went to my coach, John Thrush, and had a heart-to-heart conversation with him. Would he be able to fully commit to such an intense undertaking at this time? Honestly, having John Thrush on Team Roach was a deal-breaker for me, because there was no one whom I respected more as a coach than him.

There is just something about this man. Without a word, he commands the respect of every weightlifter who meets him, and the moment he begins coaching you, you innately know that you can trust him fully and completely. In addition, just his presence in the gym would motivate me to give my very best every single lift, every single time. Even when he was busy working with other athletes! He pushed me towards excellence, and he believed in me more than I believed in myself. I can truthfully say that had John Thrush not been a key player on Team Roach, I don't think I would've had the honor of representing my country at the 2008 Olympics. Can you see how crucial it is that you bring the "right" people onto your team?

Once we secured Coach Thrush, we asked Dr. Greg Summers, my chiropractor, if he would be able to "sign-on" to Team Roach; we needed his expertise as we dealt with my back issues from day to day. Next, we contacted Eleanor Barrager, a nutritionist who could help me understand the best foods to fuel my body with as I pushed my muscles to their limits. We asked my mom to help with the care of our children and household, and we hired very capable, goal-oriented people who could step into the management of Roach Gymnastics while our focus was toward making the Olympic team.

And now, looking back, I can honestly say that the only reason Team Roach experienced the Olympic victories we did is because we were just that: Team Roach, not merely Melanie Roach. The same will be true for you, too, as you pursue the dreams you have in your heart. The team of people you have around you will make all the difference, so when you are contemplating whom to link arms with, the most important advice I have for you is to choose wisely!

Here are three essential qualities Dan and I believe are important to identify when selecting people to be on your team:

1. Belief in the Dream

Every person who is an intricate member of your support system must honestly believe in the dream and the inevitable success of that dream. This sounds like a no-brainer, but I am always surprised when I'm talking to someone who is having issues with a staff member, or a sponsor, or a close confidante, and when I ask them if they're certain of the person-in-question's loyalty, they can't answer the question. They're not sure if the person is "all in" or just "hanging around to see if this thing works out."

Listen, if you have someone like this on your team, it's time to renegotiate your team roster! With all the time, energy, and resources you will need to give towards your goal, you cannot afford to have people around you who don't believe in you 100% or who aren't even sure if they want to be there or not. Your dream is too important. They can still be your friends; just not in the inner-workings of your project at hand.

You need to surround yourself with people who believe in you so much that they push you to be your best and will support you when you feel like giving up. For instance, during training there were days when I'd be so tired or in so much pain (or both!) that I'd go to bed without diligence to my nightly core exercises. Dan would literally push me out of bed so I would finish them, and that went on for almost a year. Let me assure you, as I stood on the Olympic platform in Beijing, I was ever-so-grateful that Dan was faithful to push me out of bed every night. Without people around you like this, you will go to bed without doing your "core work" and eventually settle for less than you dreamed. Make sure to pick team members who are so sold out to the vision that they will be relentless with you and will help push you forward to success.

2. Positive Attitude

Negativity kills creativity, motivation, and can even stop momentum. The people around you must have a positive attitude about them. Backbiting, gossiping, complaining, condescension, nagging, and bickering can have no place on your team. And let me add to the list, negative sarcasm. In our society, sarcastic humor is prevalent, but I don't appreciate it at all. Even though people will say, "Hey, lighten up; I was only joking!", the bottom line is, it's negative and over time, these types of words penetrate and make a negative impact. Attitudes like these will suck the life right out of you and spread like cancer throughout the rest of the people on your team. In addition, if your vision is far-reaching, you certainly don't want people who exude these qualities representing you or your endeavors to the press, to your clients and/or to the public.

Instead, choose people who see the glass of life as half-full, who see problems as opportunities to create solutions, and who have the ability to inspire others. The energy from these types of people will also spread through the rest of your team, but instead of bringing others down, they will foster enthusiasm and camaraderie. And, you will be proud to have these types of individuals represent you to the public, to your clients, or to your supporters.

3. Surround Yourself with the Best

Dr. Summers, my chiropractor, always says, "If you have a Maseratti and it has an engine problem, you aren't going to take it to a Hyundai dealership to get it fixed. You go to the Maseratti dealership." Likewise, if you want to be the best, you've got to surround yourself with the best. Your dream is too important to settle for mediocrity.

Here's the problem with mediocrity: if deep down in your heart, you know you settled somewhere along the journey of your dream, then if for any reason you don't reach your goals, you will be filled with regret. You'll wish you would've paid that little extra for the better employee, or researched a little more to ensure you were receiving expert advice. Conversely, if you surround yourself with excellence, and give your dream your very best shot, then no matter what, you will have no regrets. You will be able to confidently lay your head down on your pillow knowing you gave it your all.

Surround yourself with the people who are the best ones for the job. Period.

KEEPING THE "VILLAGE" ON COURSE

Once the village of your team is situated, I wish I could tell you the hardest work was complete…but I'd be lying to you. Keeping the team motivated, on the same page, and able to maintain a standard of excellence will not be easy. Impossible? No. Challenging? Absolutely! It's going to take a ton of strategizing to keep your team galvanized, but let me assure you, the work is definitely worth it. When you and your team are enjoying the journey of achieving success, everyone feels an unmatched feeling of pride and satisfaction.

Whether it's running an election campaign, or going after an Olympic dream, or up-starting and later expanding a flourishing gymnastic training center, Dan and I have spent countless hours in the area of team building. We both desire the people on our teams to be committed to us and to the goals at hand; but first, we must show our love and commitment to each and every member of our team.

Dr. Summers gives a ton of time to athletes in track and field, boxing, Olympic swimming, and professional basketball, among others. He has volunteered hundreds of hours, and donated thousands of dollars of his services. Many times he doesn't even get a thank you. And sometimes, only complaints. Both Dan and I have made special efforts to thank Dr. Summers in many ways. Everything from a simple thank you, to sending referrals, and to showing up to promote his new office.

Only by appreciating others and acknowledging their strengths will we cultivate excellent team members who are interested in engaging long-term. And while Dan and I could write entire books on the intricacies we implement to cultivate productive and cohesive teams, for the sake of time, I'll accentuate one of the cyclical strategies we consistently use: Communicate the Goal, Remind Them of the Goal, Re-assess the Journey to the Goal; Repeat.

At the beginning of the journey, and to every new team member who might join on along the way, Dan and I are diligent to communicate the carefully-laid-out dream very clearly to the team. We share the long-term goal(s) as well as the short-term ones that we'll need to accomplish step by step. We express our vision for success, and invite each member to embrace it. In addition, we take the time to help every individual understand his or her significant part in the plan, and how integral they are for the team's success.

At any point we notice the team losing focus or excellence, or we see a dip in morale, we set out to remind the team about both the short term and long term goals. Creating fresh goal points is vital. For instance, one time with Roach Gymnastics, we were at a critical point with an expansion. Dan and I recognized morale was a bit low, so we brought the team together and set before them some very specific management goals. It was amazing how they responded, rallying around every goal. People came up with creative ideas about how to achieve them, the team began to gel again, morale improved, and staff productivity increased. Everyone was focused on a set goal, and was excited to see the success of it achieved.

Then, quarterly or semiannually, it's necessary to seriously reassess the path the team is taking. Are the implemented strategies and systems still working? Are the team members still passionate about the journey? Is each team member happy and/or excelling in his or her specific job? This is not the time to be "Mr. Nice Guy," it's the time to be "Mr. Nice AND Brutally Honest Guy!" Make adjustments where needed, regroup, and then repeat the entire process.

Finally — and I did not include this as part of the above cyclical strategy because this team tactic is daily — you must make every member of the team feel appreciated. At every opportunity, speak encouragement and gratitude to the people of your 'village.' Go the extra mile to show them how much they mean to you and how important they are to the success of the entire team. Write notes. Give gifts. Have parties. Bless those that excel with monetary bonuses. As a team leader, the relationship with the members of your team must be reciprocal. If you are loyal to them, they will be loyal to you.

It's going to take a village. If the dream you are going for is important and noteworthy, while you might be able to accomplish it all by yourself, it will be much easier if you have a team around you to help. Not to mention, the enjoyment of the journey toward your dream is exponentially greater. Build your team, and in turn, your team will build you.

Seven:
When Opportunity Knocks

Photo with President George W. Bush

Chapter Seven:
WHEN OPPORTUNITY KNOCKS

I FIRMLY BELIEVE THERE IS NO LACK OF OPPORTUNITY FOR ANY PERSON. Where there is a legitimate dream, there will also be the advantageous chance to bring that dream to pass. So be encouraged! If after reading the previous chapters of this book you are more certain than ever before that your dream is the 'right' one for you to pursue, then I guarantee you, there is the opportunity available to turn your dream into reality. And if you will begin to see the landscape of your world through the eyes of possibility, you'll begin to recognize the many ways in which opportunity is knocking at the door of your life.

But just because opportunity knocks, that does not mean you'll automatically discover success. You've still got to get up off the couch and open the door! And not only that, you've got to be prepared and ready to fully embrace the opportunities when they come knocking. In my life, I've known several people who have had great dreams for their lives, dreams that because of their gifts and talents were completely within their reach, but they have never been able to actually live them out. And 9 times out of 10, it's simply because they've either not recognized true opportunity when it arises, or they had not prepared well enough and were not ready to pounce when opportunity showed itself.

If you desire to see the dream for your life come to pass (and I know you do, or you would've stopped reading this book by now), it is crucial that you understand not only how to recognize opportunity when it knocks, but also how to have positioned yourself so that you have the ability to seize it when it comes…rather than allow it to slip through your fingers. Because when great opportunities come your way and offer you the chance to realize your dreams, if you are not in a position to take advantage of that opportunity, then the decision has already been made for you. You'll be forced to watch that once-in-a-lifetime chance pass you right by. How frustrating! Let's learn how to be completely prepared to embrace every life opportunity when it knocks on our doors.

When Dan and I launched Roach Gymnastics, we really didn't have the vision for the gym to become as large as it is today. I simply had a passion for gymnastics, and wanted to create an avenue for others who shared this passion to enjoy the sport. As a young girl, I loved competitive gymnastics, and it was where my dream to become an Olympic athlete began. While it wasn't in the cards for me to fulfill a career in gymnastics, I had a desire to help other young people engage in this exciting sport. We started Roach Gymnastics with this simple goal in mind. So how have we gone, in just a few years, from teaching recreational gymnastics out of a garage to a fully outfitted 20,000+ sq. ft. facility with high-caliber gymnasts and a superior coaching staff? Only because of the opportunities that presented themselves. But, let me assure you, it wasn't just because opportunity knocked. It was because Dan and I were in a position to act when it did.

For instance, after Roach Gymnastics officially opened its first facility in 2003, we quickly grew to our full capacity. As a result, in early 2004, we completed an expansion to accommodate our growth, and in doing so, incurred many thousands of dollars of debt. While there was no urgent need to do this, Dan and I strategized the quickest way possible to pay off the expansion debt, and diligently followed through with that plan. We were so grateful we did because as soon as that debt was paid off, we were blessed with so much business, we had to either turn away the increasing numbers of young athletes, or complete another expansion in 2005. We chose the latter of the two and once again worked to pay off this new debt as quickly as possible.

We continued to grow, and by 2008, we were bursting at the seams. An opportunity presented itself for us not only to move our facility into a wonderful new location but also to complete a third expansion project. Because we were now debt-free, we were able to seize the chance and move forward. None of these expansions could've occurred if we had not been prepared (by being financially able) to pounce on these prospects.

Once again, we set out to clear our debt, and no sooner had we accomplished that, a huge break came our way. One of the best gymnastics coaches in our seven state region knocked on our door and asked us if we were looking for a head optional coach. What an incredible opportunity! The only problem was our facility was not adequately supplied with what this coach would need. If we were going to bring him aboard, that also meant another expansion (and another loan) to outfit our gym with the space and equipment necessary for the higher levels we could now train. Had we not worked so hard to pay off the debt from the previous expansions, there would have been no way we could've been in a financial position to prepare the gym for what this coach could bring to the table. We would've had to make the painstaking decision to turn him away and watch that incredible opportunity walk out the door. We were so thankful we had positioned ourselves (without even knowing it) to be catapulted to a new level of success.

Dan and I yet again worked very hard to pay down the debt we had incurred. Who knew when the next amazing business opportunity would present itself? Sure enough, the very next year, we caught wind of a nearby gym that unfortunately was going under. We knew that if that gym failed, there would be hundreds of gymnasts that would need a new gym in which to train. Dan and I thought, *All these gymnasts are going to go somewhere...why not to Roach Gymnastics?* Once we were fairly certain that gym was not going to make it, we signed a lease for an additional 10,000 sq. ft. in anticipation and planning for the growth of those new athletes. Furthermore, we filled that space with state-of-the-art competitive gymnastic equipment. It was only because we had paid down our debt that we were in a position to do this. And when that other gym closed its doors, many of those athletes moved over to Roach Gymnastics. Again, had we not been in the position to take advantage of this opportunity, we wouldn't have been able to provide the extra space and coaching for these athletes and they would've gone somewhere else to continue their sport.

Obviously, these business decisions included a lot of risk and no guarantees. But we were prepared, not only for the opportunity, but also to take those risks. Dan and I have never regretted it for a moment. If we hadn't been ready to seize these opportunities, today Roach Gymnastics would be operating out of a smaller facility, and we would be producing mediocre athletes. Don't allow yourself to be the person who misses the opportunity when it knocks! Let's spend some time talking about the reasons why most people either fail to recognize when opportunity is calling or choose to ignore the call.

WHY WE MISS OPPORTUNITY

The number one reason most people pass up great opportunities when they present themselves is because of fear. We are afraid to fail, afraid to take the risk, afraid of the unknown, afraid of _____ (you can fill in the blank). Please, let me assure you, just because Dan and I have experienced some wonderful successes in our lives does not mean we've done so without fear. If I had a dollar for every time I felt myself feeling nervous or fearful about something I was about to embark upon, I'd be rich! Who doesn't experience these feelings at times? But no matter the fears, you have to choose to be brave and take the leap of faith. Even if it means doing it afraid.

Yes, the risks are sometimes higher than we'd expected, but the bigger the dreams, the larger the risks. There's no way around that. So what do we do? After we've thought everything through and come up with a well-drawn-out plan, we must trust our gut feeling, embrace the right opportunities, and move forward, believing 100% that we are going to be successful...regardless of our feelings of fear.

Another reason people thwart opportunities is they don't want to do what it takes, a.k.a., they don't want to work hard. Someone once said, "Opportunity is often missed because it comes disguised as hard work." As I've mentioned before, it's easy to sit on the couch and dream big dreams. Really, anyone can do that. But in order to forge a new path for your life, it's most assuredly going to take sacrifice and hard work. It's going to take you stepping out of your comfort zone. If an opportunity approaches you and you find yourself thinking thoughts like, "That is going to take so much effort." or, "Wow. Surely an easier way will show itself." or, "Do I really want to work that hard?!", stop for a moment and reevaluate. Do you really want your dream to come to pass? If the answer is yes, then you've got to roll up your sleeves and get ready to dive into some hard work! Visualize a detailed picture of success until that image overshadows your desire to stay in your comfort zone.

Finally, a main reason people allow opportunities to be overlooked is because of a lack of self-confidence. They just don't believe they can do it. While their dreams tug away at their hearts, their self-doubts cloud their vision, and when an opportunity opens up to them, they talk themselves out of taking any chances. "Who am I to think I could achieve that?" "I'll probably fail anyway, so why even bother?" "I'm just not ready for that kind of success." It's human nature to think these kinds of thoughts, but if we want to enjoy the journey of our lives, we've got to fight to squelch these sabotaging fears.

If you struggle with a lack of confidence, make sure to surround yourself with close friends who believe in you. Talk about your doubts and allow them to help you learn to believe in yourself. Discuss the opportunities at hand and ask them for their brutally honest opinions and advice. Remember the earlier section on the importance of teamwork? Right here is a perfect example for how imperative a super-positive team of people around you can help you take the leap of faith even when your knees feel wobbly.

If it were easy, everyone would be doing it. So, keep your fears in check, be ready for the challenge, and squelch the doubts that try to congest your mind. You've been given the dream in your heart so that you will make it come to pass!

ENJOYING THE JOURNEY
MAKES OPPORTUNITY HAPPEN

For the last few chapters we've been unpacking the strategies and logistics of how to translate your dreams into reality. After all that cerebral content, I want to remind us of the objective of this book. It's not just to have great successes along the journey of our lives; much more importantly, my purpose for writing is to help you enjoy the journey of your life. What good is brilliant success if you are not having fun and loving your life along the way?

In Chapter Three, I wrote how important it is to enjoy each day, and I gave four crucial steps about how to do this. I'd like to use this chapter on opportunity as an example to show you just how powerful, and practical, those four steps are, because if you utilize them, they can actually help position yourself to be ready for any opportunity that comes your way. These factors aren't merely happy little thoughts to motivate you for a day or two and then become forgotten. They are so much more than that. My hope is that by showing you how they apply to this chapter, you will understand how to use these four principles as daily tools in every realm of your life, whether it be in your marriage, your parenting, your relationships, or your business.

ONE: FIND JOY

Every day, it is possible to choose joy, to see the glass as half full, to find something positive to be grateful for. It will be so difficult to enjoy the journey of your life if you have a daily deficiency of joy. A lack of joy produces pessimism, and completely blinds your eyes to opportunity. Let me explain it like this: The first time I became pregnant, it wasn't long before I began to notice all the other pregnant ladies out there. I'd go to the mall and see several pregnant women shopping. At the grocery store, there'd always be someone else pushing her cart sporting a baby bump and a t-shirt that read, "I'm not just getting fat, I'm pregnant." And at church, sure enough, more pregnant people! I remember thinking, Wow, what a coincidence that all these people are pregnant at the same time I am. And then it occurred to me. The reason I was seeing all these prego's wasn't because these women coincidentally became pregnant simultaneously with me; it was because until I was pregnant myself, I simply hadn't noticed them before. They'd always been there; they just weren't on my radar.

For all you men reading this book, it's like when you decide on the brand of car you next want to purchase. Before this, you could drive to work and not really think about how badly you wanted a new car, but now that you've narrowed down your choice to a specific model and make, you see it everywhere you go! Cruising down the highway, you see dozens of your dream car, and in every parking lot, it seems there's one in every row. Did, all of a sudden, the people around you run out and buy the exact car you wish you had? Not at all. Those cars where always there, you just are now noticing them because that model and make is in the forefront of your mind.

Joy is all around us, just like the pregnant ladies and the cars were there all the time. We simply need to look for it. When you learn to find the joy in your every day, you teach yourself to see the positive things happening around you. Optimistic thoughts are in the forefront of your mind. As a result, your eyes will be clear to recognize opportunities as they arise — even the small ones — because you are focused on seeing possibility. On the other hand, when you are full of heaviness and negative thoughts, you lose the ability to see opportunities. You'll dismiss them with the thoughts, "That'll never work anyway." Or, "Nothing that good could ever happen to me."

Discipline yourself to find joy every day. Your eyes will be opened up to recognize the many opportunities that have been waiting for you.

TWO: SAVOR LIFE

The secret to learning how to savor life is to treat every day like it was your last. To help you learn to do this, in Chapter Three I gave you these questions to ask yourself: How would I go about this day if I knew it was my last to spend with my spouse, my kids, or even just to do the things I love to do? If this were the case would the landscape of the next 24 hours change at all? Would I treat people differently? Would I waste even a moment of my last day on earth?

When you are truly savoring each day, living like it was your last, not only will you recognize opportunity when it comes a-knocking, but you will also have the discernment to know which doors of opportunity are worthwhile for you to open and which ones are just a waste of time. There are so many great, innovative ideas out there, but not all of them are expedient for the fulfillment of your dream. You must be able to discriminate between which opportunities will help you get where you want to go, and which ones will wind up being a distraction. When you are living to savor the moment, you won't allow anything to steal away your precious time, and you'll be very good at separating the great opportunities from the good ones.

THREE: LIVE IN THE MOMENT

So often, we become so busy planning for tomorrow that we forget to actually live in the now. In addition, with our fast-paced society, we run from one thing to the next, doing three things at the same time: driving while eating while talking on the phone. Or, working out while reading while listening to music. Or, hanging with the family while watching television while texting while facebooking! If we are speeding through our days like this, then we'll whiz right by the new opportunities trying to get our attention. Sometimes the greatest ideas designed to help make our dreams come true come from the most unsuspecting conversations and experiences, and it takes a quiet mind to decipher these subtle opportunities as the diamonds they are. Don't be so in a hurry for tomorrow that you forget to notice the beauties of today.

FOUR: HAVE NO REGRETS

Live your life fully, and purpose to enjoy the journey of your life. If you will do this, you will have no regrets. In addition, when you approach life with this posture, you will find the courage to seize great opportunities when they come your way. The cost of every opportunity is risk. But when you are determined to live with no regrets, you'll be ready to pay the price of risk and give your 110% to making sure you squeeze the most out of every opportunity you get.

Opportunities are out there for the taking, and somebody's going to grab them...why not have that somebody be you? Don't allow yourself to buy into the lie that the people around you who've found success were "just lucky." 99% of the time, success has nothing to do with luck. Rather, it has everything to do with the ability to recognize opportunity, to have positioned oneself to be able to seize it when it comes, and a whole lot of hard work.

Opportunity is knocking at your door...recognize it, be ready for it, and take the risk to welcome it in!

Eight:
If It Were Easy, Everybody'd Be Doing It

Melanie sitting atop the total weight she could lift!

Chapter Eight:

IF IT WERE EASY,
EVERYBODY'D BE DOING IT

Perseverance. It's a quality everyone wants to possess. The only problem is that most of us never want to face the kind of challenges that require true perseverance! We want our dreams to come true, but only if they are easily accomplished and come sooner than later. In other words, we want it (whatever that "it" is) to come easily. And to come now. Hey, I'm no different from anyone else; I'd love for everything in my life to work out perfectly the first time without me having to break a sweat or mess up my hair and makeup.

However, the fact we all know to be true is that in order to experience the success of a dream come true, it's going to take hard work and a whole lot of perseverance. One statement I find myself saying over and over to our competitive gymnasts is, "If it were easy, everyone would be doing it." I remind them that there are probably dozens of girls at their schools who wish they could be gymnasts, but the only ones who actually live out those dreams are the ones who are willing to put in the many hours of training. And of those gymnasts who are willing to sacrifice time with their family and friends, other hobbies, favorite TV shows, and the like just so they can work out for hours every day, the only ones who become champions are those who persevere through the pain, the failures, and the stress. The champions are the ones who never give up.

Whatever our dreams are: a thriving business, a strong marriage, the raising of successful children, an athletic pursuit, a weight loss goal, we can see the realization of those dreams. But not without perseverance. Webster's Dictionary defines perseverance as: "Steadfastness in doing something despite difficulty or delay in achieving success." We must be able to see our goals through, despite any challenge or setback that might come our way, even if it postpones our finish line. And the reason I'm so passionate about this can be surmised in the second definition the dictionary gives for perseverance: "Continuance in a state of grace leading finally to a state of glory." Isn't that beautiful? If we will persevere with grace through all the obstacles of our journey, eventually, we will see ourselves transformed into a state of glory!

This is what my desire is for you. This is what propels me to invest my time and resources into writing this book. I truly believe that whatever the dream is in your heart, you will be able to see it come to pass if you will remain steadfast and never give up. And, trust me, there is nothing more satisfying than experiencing the joy of persevering toward your goal...all the way until you are finally led to a state of glory, an overwhelming sense of accomplishment of a job well done.

When Dan and I made the resolve that I should go for a comeback and attempt to make it to the 2008 Olympics, we had no idea of the huge obstacles we were soon to encounter. I can honestly say, in that first year of training, 2005-2006, I was confronted with some of the darkest days—both emotionally and physically—that I'd ever faced. As a mom, I was walking through the heart-wrenching news that my son had autism, and as I described in earlier chapters, I struggled personally with this for many months. As an athlete, I battled mentally with frustration about how far I had to improve in order to qualify for the Olympic team. In addition, the pain in my back from former injuries was intense and constant.

There were many, many times I felt strong inclinations to throw in the towel and just give up. In fact, Dan and I had multiple conversations during this season where we talked about quitting, but neither one of us seemed to be able to actually say, "We're done." Inside my heart, there was a perseverance that simply would not allow me to stop. If you would've asked me while I was in the midst of it, where that internal drive came from, I probably wouldn't have had a clear explanation about the why. But now in hindsight, I can plainly recognize several factors that worked together to build the kind of perseverance I needed to push through those terribly rough months and experience the reward of victory.

BECOME REFINED, NOT DEFINED

When I began my journey as a weightlifter in the late 90s, I certainly did not possess the ability to persevere:

mentally, emotionally, or physically. To be honest, I didn't need it at first because everything came so easily. In just two years, I went from being a beginner to a world record holder, and my success was unprecedented. Ranked #1 in the US, I was favored to win a gold medal at the '98 World Championships in Lahti, Finland. An article had just come out in the USA Today proclaiming me, "The New Face to Women's Weightlifting," and my financial sponsor was chomping at the bit to publish my world record performance in their next magazine. It seemed nothing was going to stop my easy glide to the top. Very unfortunately, however, during that competition, I completely bombed out. I couldn't hold the weight and I didn't even total. It was horrible! Now, bombing out at any meet can be difficult to deal with, but to do it on a world stage with everyone expecting you to set world records and win a world championship can be devastating.

I was not ready internally to handle this kind of setback. The feeling of defeat was so thick, I let doubt come in and sear my mind with a lasting memory of my failure. As a result, I allowed this negative experience to define me as a loser instead of a winner. Mind you, I never would've admitted this at the time, perhaps I wasn't even consciously aware of it. But looking back now, I can definitely see that my dreams of being a champion had begun to become clouded with the fears of failing again, of letting my coaches down, of letting myself down. While I became more motivated than ever to train my body physically, mentally and emotionally, I was not enjoying the journey of my life!

Then the following year, after I bombed out at the Pan American Games, a 2000 Olympics qualifying event, one of my coaches said something to me that I'll never forget. I was heavily favored to win the gold medal, but during the meet I hyper-extended my elbow and was forced to sit in the stands and watch as other lifters (all of whom I'd previously beaten) take their medals. I was sitting in the back, crying, when my Pan Am team coach, Michael Cohen, walked over to me, patted my head and said, "Refiner's fire, baby. Refiner's fire." Granted, his words didn't help soothe the pain I was feeling at that moment, but as I continued to grow as an athlete, I came to understand the wisdom and the power of those words.

What is the "refiner's fire"? In order for a silversmith to create pure silver, he must put the silver through a refining fire. Taking a large piece of silver, he holds it in the middle of the fire, where the flames are the hottest, so that all the impurities can burn off. This is the only way for the silver to become pure and far more valuable than if the impurities were still intact. In essence, my coach was saying to me, "Yes, it hurts right now, but if you won't give up and instead use this situation to refine your character, you will come out of this better than before."

And so it is with our dream pursuits. When adversity comes, and the heat is turned up in our lives, so often we want to run away from the flames. It's too painful and uncomfortable to stay in that place of challenge. The only problem with running away, or avoiding the fire altogether, is that without those seasons of refining, we will never allow the impurities of our lives to be consumed by our perseverance and to eventually move forward to a place of victory. In addition, if we embrace difficult and/or negative situations with an attitude to learn and to grow, then when we come out of the refiner's fire, we'll find within ourselves a deeper confidence and an inner strength we never knew existed. Rather than being defined by our failures or by unfortunate circumstances, we can allow those very things to refine our hearts, our souls, our lives.

I didn't fully understand the benefit of the refiner's fire and how it cultivated perseverance until that day the Bishop met with me and talked with me about Drew's autism. During that meeting, I was at the lowest point of my life, emotionally, and every day I was fighting the urge to give up on everything. As I explained in Chapter 2, after this fateful conversation, my entire perspective shifted and I saw what had happened and what was happening in my life in a completely different way. Instead of being a victim of my circumstances, I began to understand that I possessed the power to embrace this (and every) situation, and to see it as positive, even if at first it seemed negative. I actually could use any adversity for my advantage to strengthen me and help me to become a better person.

Adversity is going to come your way, and it is going to take perseverance to walk through to the other side of it. Sometimes it will seem so much easier to give up or to settle for a cheap imitation of your dream, but if you yield to these temptations, you will also be passing up the opportunity to live in the vibrancy of your deepest dreams. Make a decision today to persevere instead. You can experience your dreams and enjoy the journey of your life, but it's going to take a big dose of perseverance. Here are some insights to help you cultivate perseverance.

IMAGINATION CAN TAKE YOU THERE

During the seasons when you feel yourself in the midst of the refiner's fire, make sure to take some time, every day if possible, to quiet yourself and imagine the end result of your dream. And I mean really imagine every detail: what it looks like and what it will feel like. Don't settle for a vague picture of that future event, like an old, grainy black-and-white home video. Use your imagination and take the time to develop a full-blown, colorful feature film, complete with 3-D and state-of-the-art special effects! See yourself walking around in that vision and reveling in the success of it. Allow this picture to be the carrot that helps lure you forward, step-by-step, even when it feels like you're never going to get there.

For me, there were many times, as I was lying flat on my back in excruciating pain or as I sat shivering in my daily ice bath, when I could feel myself tempted to just stop all this chaos and retreat to a "normal" life, whatever that was. But then I would imagine myself walking with Team USA during the opening ceremonies of the Olympics, and I would visualize myself standing on that Olympic platform, competing against athletes from all over the world. When I put myself inside that future dream and imagined what that would be like, my perseverance would kick in, and I'd be able to make it through another day.

Imagine the thriving business. Imagine yourself finally fitting into your dream-size jeans. Imagine walking across that stage to receive your diploma. Imagine the reward of saving for retirement. Obviously, we cannot live inside the imaginations of our mind, but we sure can use them as pick-me-ups when we feel like throwing in the towel!

YOUR TEAM CAN TAKE YOU THERE

Chapter Six was all about the importance of having a team around you who could help transform your dream into a reality. In cultivating a persevering attitude, your team will be crucial. You must be sure to surround yourself with strong, positive people because when you hit a low spot and need help, there will be someone there to pick you up and to give you the mental and emotional support you need. When resources seem slim and you begin to doubt whether you should've embarked on this journey in the first place, you need someone there to talk you out of your doubts and keep you on course.

During the years of training for my Olympic comeback, there certainly were times when I seriously doubted my body was actually going to be able to endure the constant stress I was subjecting it to. One day, I was in so much pain I could only hobble into my chiropractor's office. He could tell by the look on my face that I was feeling a bit panicky about how much longer my back would last. He looked me in the eyes and said, "Melanie, I can see that you're worried. Just remember, until you see panic in these eyes (pointing to his own), you don't need to worry. Just keep your eyes on the prize." I honestly don't know what I would've done without him. Because I trusted his skill implicitly and because I knew he was 100% dedicated to whatever was best for me, I knew I was in good hands. And this is just one example from the many when members of Team Roach would lift my spirits and help move me forward.

If, as you read this, you are feeling discouraged and ready to give up, I urge you to reach out to the people around you who love you. Even to people you might know, whom you might not be that close with, but whom have gone through a similar situation that you are in. Don't try to carry the whole load by yourself! Be proactive and ask for help. So often, we don't ask because we think we'd be burdening others with our problems, but in truth, there are many people out there who are full of knowledge and are more than happy to give advice and to help. Take a step of faith and allow someone else to encourage you and help you build your perseverance.

ENJOYING THE JOURNEY CAN TAKE YOU THERE

Are you starting to understand why the subtitle of this book is called *Enjoying the Journey of Life?* That phrase is showing up everywhere! In the last chapter, I showed you how to utilize the four steps to enjoying the journey to help you recognize opportunity. You can use them the same way with perseverance. Whenever you need to cultivate perseverance in your life, pull out those four steps, meditate on them, and apply them to this realm of life.

I won't go through each step like I did in the last chapter, but let me share this one point with you: If you can get to the place where you are truly enjoying the journey, focusing 100% on what is happening right now, you will have the perseverance to endure anything. Worrying about tomorrow erodes our ability to keep our hopes up and to believe we will eventually come to a place of victory. Regretting about our yesterdays makes us feel sorry for ourselves and sucks the life right out of an attitude of perseverance. You only have control over this moment, in this day. You've lost control of the past, and you cannot yet control the future. All you have is right now. If you can discipline yourself to enjoy each and every day, you will have the perseverance to find success, and you will never look back!

PERSEVERANCE FOR A LIFETIME

I want to take a moment to address a different level of perseverance that requires every morsel of your heart and soul. As a mother of a special needs child, I understand that some of you, like me, must face situations that in essence have no "end result" or "final victory." My Olympic career came and went, but my son, Drew, will always have autism and will most likely never live outside our home. For Dan and me, finding the perseverance to endure each day will be an ongoing challenge. Perhaps you have a special needs child. Or, perhaps you have an illness for which there is no cure.

I cannot express to you how much I wish I could give you a simple fix that you could apply to your life and then go on your merry way. But, we both know that "simple fix" does not exist. These kinds of issues aren't ones that can be solved; they are the kind that simply must be endured. For Dan and me, the only way we have found strength, peace, and joy is by using the four principles I write about in this book: Find Joy, Savor Life, Live in the Moment, and Have No Regrets. We live by them, and we use them to help keep balance and perspective in our lives. It is only because we have truly learned to enjoy the journey of each and every day, that I have the ability to offer these principles to you with such confidence. If they worked for us, they will most assuredly work for you, too.

The first thing we must understand is that the timeframe for our dreams and goals is different than, say, an Olympic one. My Olympic dream had a hard timeline, and I was able to gear up (and change up) our lives to accommodate the allotted span of time it required. In dealing with Drew and his autism, Dan and I know we need to approach this situation as a marathon, not a sprint. Let me remind you of Webster's definition of perseverance: "Steadfastness in doing something despite difficulty or delay in achieving success." I cannot think of a more accurate picture of these words than one of a parent raising a special needs child. Especially when that child will have his or her special need for their entire lifetime here on earth.

For Dan and me, there are stretches of time (sometimes, painstakingly long ones) when the challenges of autism are extremely difficult and it is sheer endurance that keeps us moving forward. During these times, we keep our perseverance up by knowing "the slow and steady win the race," and it's all about never giving up, always putting one step in front of the other. We set long-term goals, as they pertain to parenting Drew, but we keep most of our focus on the day-to-day, survival/routine. Because this journey will be a life-long one, we are extremely conscious to maintain balance in our marriage and with our other children by establishing routines that can be sustained over the years.

For me, I rely on the help of good friends, and most of all, I lean into my relationship with God to carry me through. And to this day, God has never failed me. However, maybe religion is not your thing. But let me assure you, you must have something that can help you settle your heart and revitalize you when you are down.

You cannot do this alone, and you need something that can fill the sails of your soul when you feel adrift in an enormous ocean of emotional endurance. Whatever your "higher power" is, make sure you carve the time into your schedule to recharge your spirit, mind, and body.

Dreams come in all shapes and sizes, and no two are exactly alike. But there is one common ingredient in the recipe to make all dreams a reality. The dreamer must be prepared to persevere through the hard work and the challenges that inevitably accompany the vision or goal. You can do it! Decide to never give up on your dream until you see it come to pass!

Nine:
When You've Done Everything Right & It Still Goes Wrong

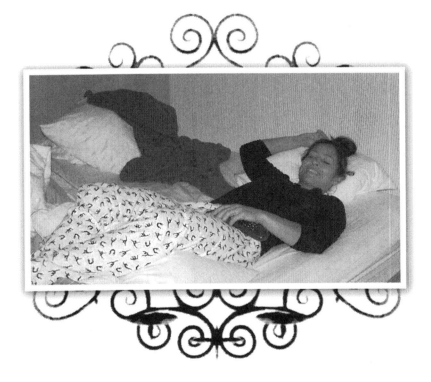

Recovering from back surgery

Chapter Nine:
WHEN YOU'VE DONE EVERYTHING RIGHT...
AND IT STILL GOES WRONG

I CAN'T BELIEVE THIS IS HAPPENING, I thought, as I rolled out of my hotel bed. After all the work I've done over these last three years; how is it that out of all those days this is the one that I wake up with the flu?! It was the morning of the 2008 Nationals in Columbus, Ohio, and this was the meet where I should finally clench my spot on the 2008 US Olympic Team. And I had a full-blown case of the flu.

I'm sure you've had the flu at least once in your life, so you know how terrible it feels. You're feverish and nauseous, your muscles ache, and your legs start shaking simply from the efforts of walking downstairs to get yourself a glass of orange juice. Now imagine feeling this way on the day of a life-changing weightlifting meet, in which you are supposed to clean & jerk twice your own body weight!

As I shuffled into the bathroom to shower and get ready, I heard myself think, I was totally prepared for this meet, to reap the harvest of all the excruciatingly hard work and all the sacrifices I've made...and my whole family has made, for that matter. What if I totally bomb out today, all because I caught the stupid flu? It just doesn't seem fair! And as soon as I heard that last thought pop in my head, I caught myself. I had come way too far in my journey to let that one take hold of my heart. Since when has Life promised to be "fair"? I reminded myself.

Regardless of how I felt physically, I knew what I needed to do, and "feeling sorry for myself" was definitely not on that list. I needed to prepare for this meet the way I always did, even with the flu, and take my turns on the platform moment by moment. Whatever was going to happen was going to happen, and Team Roach would have to deal with the results accordingly. I prayed that the Lord would be my strength (literally), and I got myself ready to compete in the 2008 Nationals.

At the end of the day, I only made 2 out of my 6 lifts, and my performance was not very good at all. While I did take first place in my weight class, that unfortunately was not what I came there to accomplish, because despite winning the Nationals, my performance did not qualify me for the Olympic team. This was a huge blow for the entirety of Team Roach. Up until this point, we had meticulously done everything right. We'd worked our tails off and made extreme sacrifices; we'd invested the bulk of our time and resources for this goal; we'd crossed all our T's and dotted all our I's, and we still did not succeed in what we came to achieve.

And so I had to face one of those unwanted truths of life. Sometimes, even when you do everything in your power and might to make your dream come to pass, there may be times when things still aren't going to work out.

I'm sure, if you've experienced this truth, you are keenly aware that it is one tough pill to swallow. There's just no way to describe the helplessness you feel when you have poured every ounce of yourself into a dream, only to have the rug pulled out from underneath you as you face the divorce papers, or the financial upheaval, or the doctor's report, or the death of a loved one, or for me personally, the flu at Nationals...or monumentally more impacting, the day I learned the prognosis of autism for my 2-year-old son. The emotions are grueling and the disappointment in your gut is like an avalanche.

This chapter is not meant to belittle or invalidate the emotions one feels when confronted with unexpected and seemingly unfair adversity. These feelings are real, and they must be acknowledged and dealt with. However, once the initial impact of the situation begins to fade, no matter what kind of challenge it is, there is one common decision that confronts every one of us: What am I going to do now? And this is the response I want to address in this chapter; because how we answer this question determines the course of our future. How we decide to proceed from the point of disappointment, whether it is big or small, will set the course for our successes in the future.

Many people who have come face-to-face with the pain and disappointment that comes from these types of undeserved situations struggle with the effects of bitterness, unforgiveness, feelings of failure, anger, resentment, and the like, and honestly believe they have no option to feel any other way. Because of the lot that's been handed to them in this life, they are who they are, and they feel the way they feel, because of it. And that's "just the way it is." But the truth is, this isn't entirely true. Sure, it's normal human nature to feel the anger or sadness or pain from a major disappointment; however, when we allow those emotions to remain in our hearts and to dictate the quality of our future, we've now become enslaved to those feelings. We're in bondage to them, and we've given up control of our dreams.

There is another answer. Yes, sometimes we have no control over what happens to us, but we always have the choice of how we will respond to it. Obviously, the shock or the pain of a circumstance is sincere, and we must allow ourselves to experience it and to grieve whatever it is we have lost...but eventually, we must focus our eyes back upwards and begin to take steps forward. The valleys of failure and disappointment are no place to set up camp! It's only when we decide to walk through those valleys that we will come to new, open fields of possibility.

CRY IF YOU NEED TO, AND THEN MOVE ON

After I received my awards for winning the 2008 Nationals, I went back to my hotel room and cried. Kind of ironic, really. Probably any of the other girls at that meet would've been celebrating after winning the Nationals, but I couldn't enjoy the win knowing I still hadn't qualified for the Olympic team.

And then, several minutes later, I made the best decision I could have. I brushed myself off, and started to strategize my next steps. Hope for the Olympic Team was not completely lost; in eight weeks, I could compete in the Olympic Trials. If I attended this and performed exceptionally, there was still a chance I could make Team USA. Team Roach regrouped and carefully took control of the only thing we could: the next eight weeks. My mindset was, I won't settle for this! I simply will not accept it. I've come too far and sacrificed too much to be beaten now. I'm going to work harder than I ever have before, and I'm going to compete better than I've ever competed. And instead of allowing this negative circumstance to define me, I allowed it to refine me. (Remember that point from the previous chapter?) I could've let this failure break me mentally, but I alternatively made the choice to let it motivate me and propel me forward. It worked! Eight weeks later, I competed excellently and finally secured my spot on the Olympic team. In just three months, I would be traveling to Beijing to be a competitor at the 2008 Olympics!

The satisfaction I felt at the Trials as I clenched my spot on Team USA was indescribable. But for the purposes of this chapter, I don't want to get lost in the telling of the success of that event because the real nugget of wisdom— and the one I want to focus on—happened eight weeks earlier. It was at the point of decision when I sat in my Columbus, Ohio, hotel room crying about my failure at the Nationals. More specifically, at the moment I decided to embrace that negative situation and make it be a positive one. Just like I introduced in the previous chapter, simply because Life has handed you a negative situation, you are not a victim of it. Rather, you have the power to make that negative thing become a positive thing.

I'm taking the time to really spell this out for you because it's one of the greatest pearls of wisdom I have learned as I've searched to enjoy the journey of my life. As a young athlete, I never would've possessed the capacity, mentally or emotionally, to handle the disappointment of not making the Olympic team at the 2008 Nationals. At this time of my athletic career, I struggled with letting a challenge like this dictate my performance in future meets because I simply couldn't let go of the visions of my past failures. As a result, my experience at the 2008 Nationals probably would've been a catalyst to a long line of subsequent bomb-outs on the competition platform.

The only difference between the 2008 Melanie and the athletically-gifted-late-90s Melanie was that I had learned through experience how to view ALL experiences, positive or negative, as positive. And luckily (tongue-in-cheek) I have had a ton of failed experiences from which to draw to make me stronger in this area: As a very young woman, I faced a failed marriage and was divorced by age 23. Shortly after, I was fortunate enough to meet Dan, and in our first months of dating was when we experienced my awful bomb-out at the '98 Finland World Championships, and his loss of his first political election. In '99, I failed at the Pan Am Games; in 2000, I failed to make the Olympic team; and then I struggled with significant weight and eating issues, only to overcome them and then face painful injury after even-more-painful injury. As you can see, I've had a lot of experience with handling disappointment.

And then the most catastrophic one of all...the day I learned my son had autism. While I had done my best with all the past negative experiences that had come my way, this one was the proverbial back-breaker. As I have already shared in this book, this experience was the one that broke me to the core and almost overwhelmed me. I'll never forget those nights kneeling at the foot of Drew's bed, praying for a recovery that never happened. Emotionally, I had hit rock bottom and I wanted to give up. I probably would have, at least internally, had it not been for the meeting with my Bishop where the light illuminated in my heart and I realized the most powerful truth that I had a choice to decide how I felt. I began to understand that I held the power to decide what sort of perspective through which I would view my circumstances. I could see the negative as negative, and give in to the emotion of it all, or I could see the negative as a positive and grow stronger from it.

Let me stress this fact: Had I not learned this crucial lesson of life, I'm not sure I ever would've forged on with my attempt to go for the 2008 Olympics. More importantly, I'm not even sure I would've moved on enough to have another child, let alone two. I would've stayed in my anguish and disappointment, I would've allowed my vision for the future to become cloudy, and I certainly would not be enjoying the journey of my life. I would've settled for "surviving the journey of my life."

Please don't settle for survival when enjoyment is available for you! Sometimes it seems easier to just stay in survival mode, but the truth is, it's ultimately much harder to endure that day after day. Instead, let's learn to look up and begin to see the positive in every situation so that we can walk through the valley of survival into a wide-open pasture of enjoyment.

TURNING THE NEGATIVE INTO A POSITIVE

Challenges are going to come. Adversity is going to intersect our life...even when we've done everything perfectly to achieve our goal. Simply so that we aren't knocked off course from shock, we need to expect that as we go for our dreams, we are bound to hit some potholes and speed bumps, some traffic delays, some dead-ends, and even some surprise detours that take us places we'd never expected. Then, when they happen, we can allow ourselves to become filled with road rage and lose our enjoyment altogether, or we can choose to turn the negative situation into a positive one. Someone once said, "When Life gives you a hundred reasons to cry, show Life you have a thousand reasons to smile." Let's let this be our motto as we learn to enjoy the journey of our lives. Here's a few simple ways to help you turn every negative situation into a positive one.

Visualize the Eternal Perspective. This life on earth we are privileged with is only part of our eternal journey. When you stop for a moment and truly consider this, it will help you discern the scope of what you are facing. I know that God has a plan and a purpose for my life. Not just for my earth walk, but also for my eternal journey with Him. I believe God, out of His great love for us, gives us our trials because He wants us to be the best we can be.

I consider each trial a gift, not a punishment, because it is designed to stretch me, to help me grow, and to make me a stronger person.

I need to be honest with you; when I am in the midst of a strong challenge, this perspective is certainly not the one that comes to my heart easily. I have to remind myself of this over and over. I tell myself again and again that God loves me, He has a plan for me, and He wouldn't give me something I couldn't handle. I just need to fully trust Him, understanding He always knows what is best for me. I ask myself how this challenge can make me better and improve my character. Sometimes, I'll even go back and read through old journals to remember how I've overcome past struggles, and to see if there is anything there that could help me with my current situation. I look back at all I've gained and learned from my past, and this helps me get out of my head for a moment and take a look at the big, eternal picture of my life. Once I can take a step back from my current hurt and disappointment, I am able to assess what is really going on and what the best choices are for me.

Forgive. Perhaps your present situation isn't one where this applies, but learning to forgive is a quality we all need for our lives, especially if we want to enjoy our journey. Somewhere along the line, someone is going to hurt us, to disappoint us, and to fail us, and we must choose to forgive. And forgive quickly. Because the truth is, whether or not the person who hurt you is sorry, the only one who suffers from unforgiveness is the person who cannot extend it. Harboring unforgiveness is like inviting a cancer into your soul, and it will eat away at your dreams and your enjoyment of life until there is nothing left but pain and bitterness. In his book, *Growing Strong in the Seasons of Life*, Charles Swindoll offers a gripping picture of the disease of unforgiveness:

Bitterness seeps into the basement of our lives like run-off from a broken sewer pipe. Every form of ugliness begins to float to the surface of those murky waters: prejudice and profanity, suspicion and hate, cruelty and cynicism. There is no torment like the inner torment of bitterness, which is the by-product of an unforgiving spirit. It refuses to be soothed, it refuses to be healed, and it refuses to forget. There is no prison more damaging than the bars of bitterness that will not let the battle end.

Regardless if the person has ever expressed his or her remorse, do yourself a great favor and forgive them…and then let it go and move on.

Sometimes, it is ourselves who we must forgive. We find ourselves in a challenge only to come to the realization that we thought we'd done everything right, but in reality, we'd overlooked some crucial elements. Maybe we chose to trust someone whom now we can plainly see was not trustworthy, and we're kicking ourselves for it. Maybe we made excuses and really didn't give it our all, so we're feeling like huge failures. Maybe we waited to long and our window of opportunity has now shut. Whatever the case may be, forgive yourself. We all make mistakes! So do your best to learn from yours so you won't repeat them… and then let it go and move on.

Focus on Your Have's, not Your Have-Not's. This one is probably the hardest because when our lives have been slammed with challenge, the last thing we seem to want to do is search for the silver lining. However, if we are only able to see our situation as negative, then it will be impossible to ever turn it around for our good. When I think back to 2000, when I failed to qualify for the Olympic team because of a herniated disk, I hated how it felt to sit in the stands and watch the other girls take their places instead of me. But once I was back at home, I decided to focus away from what I didn't achieve and look toward the positives that I did possess: I still had a wonderful husband and we were starting a great business, and Dan was enjoying a successful political career. And soon after, we got pregnant with our first child. Had I made the Olympic team that year, who knows when Dan and I would've decided to start a family? When I look at my oldest son, I am reminded about how very possible it is to turn a negative situation into a wonderful one!

If you need to, make a list of everything that is good in your life. Are you healthy? Can you walk? Are you prosperous enough that you have clothes on your back and you eat your meals indoors? If you were able to add these to your list, do you even understand how fortunate you are, compared to the rest of the world? Do you have living family members and friends whom you love? Do you live in a country that doesn't oppress women and children? Are you free to make decisions for your life? Again, count your blessings! While these may seem trivial to you, if you had any of these taken away, you would immediately recognize how extremely valuable and important these aspects of life are to you.

As parents of a child with autism, both Dan and I have had to mentally fight to keep our mindsets in the "have's" of Drew's life and future, instead of the "have-not's." True, we struggle day-to-day with the affects of his disability. But he still can walk, feed himself, and communicate his basic needs. Some days he shows forward progress, and we celebrate those days. There are parents whose daily situation with their child is much worse, whose autistic child has never shown improvement. And I also know some other parents who, because of sickness, disease, or a terrible tragedy, have lost their children altogether. I cannot imagine the grief of going through those life situations.

Every person who walks on this earth is going to encounter tough situations and major disappointments at some time or another. Even when we have done everything in our power to "win" or to avoid it. Just because we've checked every box on our list, dotted all our I's and crossed all our T's, does not guarantee we will always win the gold medal. But should that be an excuse to not be diligent? Of course not! Our diligence to do everything in our power to make our dreams come true will enable us to never have any regrets. I can honestly say that if, in the end, I had not made the 2008 Olympic team, there is not one thing I could've identified that I would have done differently. The entirety of Team Roach had done our very best on all points and had carried out every strategy we knew to do. We gave it everything we had. I can say this with certainty because as I competed in Beijing, I surprisingly realized that making the Olympic team wasn't the thing that gave me my greatest satisfaction. It was the actual journey, the day-to-day grind, the overcoming of the impossible odds to make my comeback, the enduring of the setbacks, and the celebration of the small victories. Standing on the platform in Beijing and setting new American records was just the icing on the cake.

No matter what disappointment you might be facing, make the life-changing decision to turn it into a positive. Yes, you might have done everything right, and it all still went wrong, but don't let that be the end of your legacy. Cry if you need to, and then brush yourself off, stand back up, and get on with your life. Learn from any mistakes, and allow the situation to make you stronger. Remember, "When Life gives you a hundred reasons to cry, show Life you have a thousand reasons to smile." Let that be the end of your legacy!

Ten:
After the Music Fades

Chapter Ten:
AFTER THE MUSIC FADES

THE FIRST FEW WEEKS AFTER RETURNING HOME from the Beijing Olympics were weird. Almost surreal. I remember walking around my house in a daze, not quite sure what to do with myself. For the last three years, my daily life had kept a tight, disciplined regimen, and each morning, I'd wake up with a very specific set of goals I knew I'd need to accomplish in order to inch me closer to making the Olympics. Now that the Games were completed, I no longer was bound by such a detailed agenda and I was free to do whatever I wanted. And I was at a loss! Think about this for a minute: experts say it takes 21 days of a repeated, regulated action to form a habit. Well, for the last 1,095+ days, I had repeated a systematic schedule and I had formed way more than a habit; I had dug a well-established rut as deep as the Grand Canyon! From 2005 until the end of the 2008 Games, my life had revolved around fulfilling the Olympic Dream. Every day was filled with a stringent workout, carefully measured meals, a massage, a nap, core work, an ice-bath, and a strict bedtime. Now that the Olympics were over, I could eat whenever I wanted, go to bed whenever I wanted, and work out whenever I wanted. The pursuit was over. Just like that.

At first I handled the transition well. That year was an election year for Dan; as a result, just weeks after Beijing, we were heavily occupied with campaigning. In addition, Roach Gymnastics was waiting for me to step back into leadership and management. And most importantly, my family had me back, had my full attention, and had my time. These components helped a great deal, but after a few months, when all of these realms of my life settled back into 'normal', I was still left sensing a void. I felt lost, and I really began to struggle internally. It seemed as if I had no specific goal to wake up to each morning, and I felt as if my purpose had become undefined. To make matters worse, I had quit lifting cold turkey, hadn't picked up a weight since I'd returned home from the Olympics. While I wouldn't call it full-on depression, I definitely was in a funk.

Many, if not all, Olympic athletes deal with this letdown, and for some, it can evolve into serious depression. It's particularly difficult for the athletes who are single, who don't own businesses or who don't have significant activities outside their sport, because once they return home, they have nothing major upon which to turn their focus. But this kind of post-success slump doesn't merely affect Olympians; it can cast a shadow over any person who has held an intense single-purposed goal for a period of time, who has worked hard, and who has invested his or her life into seeing that goal come to pass. A businessperson after a huge deal. A parent raising a crew of children and now they're all in school, or even more intense, the last one has just left for college. An actor at the end of a huge production. A person who just beat a long battle with cancer. A person who has just retired from a long successful career.

There have been countless books written about how to overcome a setback or a failure, how to stand back up from the ash heap, dust yourself off, and move on. However, I think it's just as challenging to move on after a huge success, after accomplishing a goal you've sweated blood and tears to make happen. What do you do with yourself after you've driven full-throttle for so long and you've finally crossed the finish line? To simply kick your car back into cruise control seems so anti-climactic, doesn't it? Post-success, there is oftentimes a vacuum created and a profound emptiness felt that is caused by the absence of a goal at hand. This after-the-music-fades season is often overlooked from our conversations because, "You've just successfully accomplished x, y, and z, so surely you can handle the afterglow, right?"

Not right. Many personal and private failures have happened in the weeks and months following a person's greatest triumphs because of an inability to handle the effects of success. Especially those that accompany even the smallest degree of public recognition. A short trip through any era of history will reveal stories of great political leaders, athletes, movie stars, and business people who possessed the superior gifting to catapult them to the top of their field, but then afterwards, they lacked the internal fortitude to keep them on top. As we go for our dreams, let's make sure that we don't also fall into this trap. Just as we need strong, dedicated plans to climb and summit our mountains, we also need drawn out plans to help keep our footing upon our descents back down the mountain!

We can underestimate how vulnerable we usually are right after a major victory. And when I say "major" victory, please don't think that simply because your exploits weren't covered by your local news stations that they aren't major. Successfully completing potty training is major. Finishing that night class while being a single parent is major. Overcoming the addiction of nicotine is major. Anything that you've spent your time and resources accomplishing, even the goals many people won't notice can leave you feeling exhausted, both physically and emotionally. Consequently, you can be left feeling quite susceptible to the post-success blues. There have been many times that either Dan or I (and sometimes simultaneously) has experienced the feelings of void that lurk after accomplishing a big goal. Through the years, we've been able to discover some effective methods to make sure that after we've reached a summit, we don't slip way down into a valley. This chapter is dedicated to helping you map a strategy to navigate through the season you will encounter after you've reached your goals.

TAKE A BREATH, REWARD YOURSELF

The first thing Dan and I usually do after any significant undertaking is plan some type of break. Whether it's time for just us two to spend a weekend together, or it's a complete family vacation, we both feel it's very important to schedule in some rest and relaxation after a project or goal is complete. In the case of the 2008 Olympics, we decided to invest in a family trip to Hawaii. It was a wonderful, refreshing vacation filled with saturated family time as we played together non-stop for over a week. While a trip like this isn't an annual norm for our household, after three years of such focus and intense work, we wanted to reward ourselves and our children for the sacrifices we'd all made during this season.

Make it a priority to take a break. It doesn't have to be immediately following the completion of a major project, but don't let too much time pass before you reward yourself; otherwise, it's likely you'll simply move on to the next thing. Many of us are so in love with the exhilaration of the summit, we can't wait for the next mountain to conquer. Trust me, I totally can relate. The momentum from the success can fool us into thinking we are superheroes and have the capacity to dive right into an even greater exploit. But the truth is, if we keep going from thing to thing, without stopping to allow our bodies, minds, and emotions to refuel and refresh, eventually we will burn out. Something will fail: our marriage, our health, our finances, our relationships, or our emotions. And it's just not worth it. Stop. Rest. Enjoy the Journey!

REFINE, NOT DEFINE

Earlier in this book we talked about how to not let failure and disappointment define us, but rather, how to use those situations to refine us. I cannot stress to you the importance of using this same strategy with success and promotion. I'm so thankful I did not reach my Olympic dream back in 2000 when I attempted it for the first time. I simply didn't possess the internal character to have handled that kind of success, and I most definitely would have allowed all the press and the accomplishment to define who I was. I would've considered myself "Melanie Roach, the Olympic Athlete" instead of who I really was, "Melanie Roach, the woman, the wife, the mom, the friend, the business owner, and the athlete who happened to work hard enough to make it to the Olympics." Do you see the difference? I was an athlete at the Olympics for just a few days, but I'm all these other things 24/7. And in 2008, it was a whole lot easier to not let this event define me because I was competing in Beijing one day and the very next changing poopy diapers and washing laundry!

It's so easy to allow success to go to our heads, and if we're not careful, we will become prideful as we consider ourselves more highly than we ought to. Just like the low points don't define us; neither do the high points. We must have the mindset that this bit of success was a moment in our lives, and now that moment has passed. We are to take all that we've learned and incorporate those truths into the person we are evolving into as we apply this wisdom into all other aspects of our lives. The truth is, it wasn't that "moment" that created us to be who we are, anyway. It's all the experiences leading up to it: the courage to step out, the hard work, the mistakes, the perseverance, and the failures. In addition, we must remind ourselves that it most likely was not we alone who accomplished the feat. It was an entire support team around us who helped us climb to the top. Never, ever forget that.

After the Olympics, when I'd tell my story, sometimes a person would say, "Oh my Goodness! You are so amazing!" To which I would quickly respond, "No really. I'm just like you. I struggle with kids, laundry, cleaning house, just like everyone else. It just so happens my gifting is one that comes with public recognition." No matter how "big" you get, as far as society would label you, never forget who you are, where you came from, and the personal integrity that helped you rise to the top. Which brings us to...

GIVE BACK

Success is a gift to be shared. It is never meant to be hoarded or to be kept to oneself. That would be like taking the time and effort to prepare a huge feast and then selfishly trying to eat the whole thing all by yourself. All you end up with is an enormous case of indigestion! After you've achieved great dreams, it is of the utmost importance to give back into the lives of others, not only for them, but also for you, too. It helps you stay grounded. It satisfies your soul, sometimes even to a deeper capacity than the actual accomplishment did. And it most definitely keeps you from slipping into the post-success blues. So, once you find success, bottle up all that you've learned and help someone else discover their own success.

Since the 2008 Olympics, I have had the opportunity to give into the lives of others by sharing my story to people from all walks of life. I cannot express how rewarding it has been to have people tell me that just from hearing about my comeback, about our journey with autism, and about how we've built a successful business, that they have been inspired to go for their own dreams. I don't think there is anything more humbling than being used by God to help another person achieve their dreams. This is the very reason why Dan and I have committed so much of our resources to write this book. If we can help just one person not give up, just one person to challenge the odds and go for their dream, or just one family deal with the challenges of autism, it will have all been worth it.

No matter what realm in which you have found success, you have something to offer another person. My friend, Ryan, has battled severely with leukemia. He had to receive a bone marrow transplant, and is now in recovery. Everything looks great for him and his future. Just at the time of writing this book, my hometown mayor had just been diagnosed with the exact form of leukemia Ryan had. As soon as Ryan found out, he was frantic in his efforts to get in touch with the mayor because he had something few people had: his experience. He was able to talk with the mayor, and offer him the kind of support, hope and encouragement that only he could give. What a precious gift! Ryan was able to use his own painful challenge and success to help someone else, and I'm sure he will have many more opportunities to do so in the course of his lifetime.

Don't hoard your success or keep it a secret. Never underestimate how valuable your experience may be to someone else. Pay it forward and give back into the lives of others.

SET NEW GOALS

Once you've rewarded yourself, taken the proper rest to clear your mind, put your current success in its proper place, and given back into the lives of those around you… it's time to set new goals! The final step to help battle the post-success blues is to look forward into the horizon of your life and search for new conquests. And don't box yourself in; your next set of goals doesn't have to be even in the same realm as your past successes.

For Dan and me, we decided to shift our goal setting completely away from weightlifting, as we decided to become pregnant with Baby #4! I mentioned earlier in this chapter that even a few months after Beijing, I was still struggling with finding a razor sharp focus and purpose for the next season of my life. Let me tell you, there's nothing like a positive pregnancy test to remedy that. Once I began to set new short-term and long-term goals, as far as being a wife and mom, the fog began to clear, and I began to climb out of my funk. I had a desire to help my five-year-old read better, to pour into parenting Drew as we walked through autism together, and to reassure my children that they were top priority in my life. There will come a day when they won't ask me to play with them anymore, and so I'm going to live everyday with them as though it is my last. No regrets!

What are the items on your bucket list? What are the dreams you know you will eventually regret if you never try to make them come to pass? Brainstorm those goals, and write them down. Evaluate which one is the best for you to pursue next, and then go for it! Use the courage you've gained from the accomplishments of everything you've achieved up until this point, and reach for the stars. Begin reading from the beginning of this book, and use these strategies for success to help you map out your new conquest. Remember, as long as your heart is beating, there are more wonderful dreams to discover and countless more opportunities to enjoy the journey of your life!

Epilogue:
Melanie Roach,
on True Greatness

The Roach Family:
Ethan, Camille, Dan, Drew, Melanie, Baby Lily, & Charlie

Epilogue
TRUE GREATNESS

You have greatness inside of you. No matter who you are, where you've come from, what your past holds, or what situations are staring you in the face at the moment, you have the potential to do great things and to be a great person. What exactly does it mean to be great? Well, that's for each individual to work out for oneself. But I can tell you this: it doesn't mean being the president of the United States, or discovering the cure for a worldwide epidemic, or even being an Olympian. Your personal greatness is found when you've discovered how to be the very best version of YOU that you can possibly be...and learned how to enjoy the journey along the way.

If you will embrace the principles in this book and practice them in your everyday life, you will begin to experience life more fully and vividly than before. Remember, it's all about perspective, so even in the valleys, you have the power inside of you to choose to see the positive and find joy, to savor life and live in the moment, and to squeeze the most out of each day so that you will never have any regrets. Some days will be easier than others to do this, but every day, it is possible.

I mentioned in the first chapter how writing this book happened to coincide with some major life transitions in both family and business, and that Dan and I had to make several difficult decisions. I cannot tell you how much this book project helped us both as we walked through those months. We were reminded of how far we'd come, of the strategies we used to find victory in former tough situations, and most of all, how effective and powerful the principles expressed in this book truly are. For this reason, I cannot stress enough the fact that this book isn't simply a "read once and then forget about it" kind of book. It actually is a manual filled with tools to help you walk through any situation in life. Keep it on hand, and read or skim through it periodically to help these truths stay fresh in your mind and heart.

I would also recommend using the extra pages we've provided to keep a journal of your thoughts and personal revelations. Write down the adversities you've faced along with an honest assessment of how you've survived them. While I never advise anyone to constantly relive past struggles over and over in one's mind, I also don't believe these instances in our lives should be easily forgotten. Having an account of these times can be very encouraging, especially when you feel yourself once again confronted with a shadowy valley. By reading them, you can go back and remind yourself how you have felt and dealt with things in the past. You'll remember how strong you have been, how long you've been able to endure, and maybe most significantly, that this time of being in the valley will not last forever. There will be an end, and you will have persevered.

Also write down the dreams you've accomplished, both big and small, how you achieved them (the good, the bad and the ugly), and how it felt to see them come to pass. And then take some time to daydream and write down the dreams still lingering in your heart, waiting to be made real. Any time you begin to doubt the possibilities of these new dreams, read about how you've been able to see others come to fruition, and you will feel your hope start to rise.

Anything is possible, and I want you to know I believe in you. There is greatness within you waiting to be unleashed, and this book will help you unlock your true potential. Remember, if you can imagine it, you can achieve it, so...

Pick a Dream,

and GO FOR IT!

About the Author

About the Author

As an aspiring young gymnast, Melanie Roach's commitment to excellence took her all the way to the Washington State High School Championships, but an injury sidelined her from the competition. Rehab included her introduction to free weights and soon thereafter a future and powerful star was in the making.

Shattering the stereotypical body image of weightlifters, the petite former gymnast quickly made it clear that strong things come in small packages. In 1996 Melanie Roach made the personal commitment to pursue her potential in weightlifting to the fullest and set her sights on the 2000 Olympic Games. She soon thereafter stunned the weightlifting world by exceeding the world standard in the clean and jerk at the 1998 US National Championships. Melanie Roach had become the #1 ranked US weightlifter and the first one in history to clean and jerk more than twice her body weight. She was poised for a 2000 Olympic debut. Devastatingly, weeks before the Olympic Trials competition Melanie Roach suffered a serious back injury. Her Olympic dreams, along with any future in the sport, appeared to be suddenly over.

With her athletic career in shambles and apparently behind her, Melanie picked herself up and moved on. She put her energy into assisting her husband, Dan, in his election to the Washington State House of Representatives, opened her own business (Roach Gymnastics), and had three children. All the while Melanie still yearned to compete.

In the summer of 2005, Melanie decided that it's never too late to chase your dreams. At 30 years old, she returned to competitive weightlifting. Despite major setbacks, including her second son being diagnosed with autism, and undergoing back surgery, she made an improbable and inspiring comeback and qualified for the 2008 Olympic games in Beijing, China. Melanie placed 5th in the 117lbs. weight class, setting personal and American records with a two lift total of 425.6 lbs.

In addition to running her business and family, Melanie is a motivational speaker. If you would like to book her for your event, please contact her at melanieroach@comcast.net.

Dan and Melanie Roach reside in Bonney Lake, Washington with their five children.

My Lift Journal

My Lift Journal

My Lift Journal

My Lift Journal

My Lift Journal

My Lift Journal

My Lift Journal

My Lift Journal

My Lift Journal

My Lift Journal

My Lift Journal

_____
_____
_____
_____
_____
_____
_____
_____
_____
_____
_____
_____
_____
_____
_____
_____
_____
_____
_____
_____
_____
_____
_____
_____
_____
_____
_____
_____

My Lift Journal

Made in the USA
Charleston, SC
24 November 2012